UNDERSTANDING SUICIDE

A National Epidemic

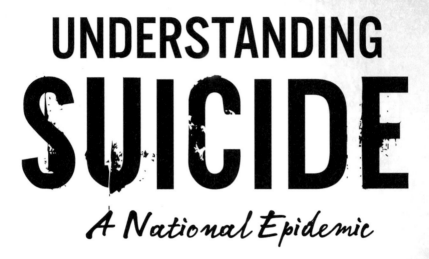

CONNIE GOLDSMITH

TWENTY-FIRST CENTURY BOOKS / MINNEAPOLIS

The author wishes to thank the following individuals for their contributions to this work:

Special thanks to Amanda Lipp, who devoted a great deal of her time and energy to this project, and to Libba Bray, Caleb Cage, e.E. Charlton-Trujillo, Chris Crutcher, Laurette Gaberman, Ann Steiner, and to all those who shared their deeply personal stories with me.

Twenty-First Century Books
A division of Lerner Publishing Group, Inc.
241 First Avenue North
Minneapolis, MN 55401 USA

For reading levels and more information, look up this title at www.lernerbooks.com.

Main body text set in Adobe Garamond Pro 11/15
Typeface provided by Adobe Systems.

Library of Congress Cataloging-in-Publication Data

Names: Goldsmith, Connie, 1945– author.
Title: Understanding suicide : a national epidemic / by Connie Goldsmith.
Description: Minneapolis : Twenty-First Century Books, [2017] | Includes bibliographical references and index.
Identifiers: LCCN 2015036216 | ISBN 9781467785709 (lb : alk. paper) | ISBN 9781512411423 (eb pdf : alk. paper)
Subjects: LCSH: Suicide—United States—Juvenile literature. | Suicide—United States—Prevention—Juvenile literature. | Suicidal behavior—United States—Juvenile literature.
Classification: LCC HV6548.U5 G66 2017 | DDC 362.28—dc23

LC record available at http://lccn.loc.gov/2015036216

Manufactured in the United States of America
1 – VI – 7/15/16

CONTENTS

Suicide is the tenth-leading cause of death in the United States, where one person dies by suicide every thirteen minutes.

Chapter 1

A CHILD LOST:
COPING WITH A LOVED ONE'S SUICIDE

Susan Caldwell knew something was wrong when her seventeen-year-old daughter didn't show up at her dad's house after school one January afternoon. "At the time, Amy was in her senior year of high school. She went to school in the morning and to a day treatment program for teens in the afternoon," Susan says. "But the program was closed for staff meetings that day, so Amy agreed to go to her dad's house after school instead. I planned to pick her up when I got off work." But Amy wasn't at her dad's house. And she didn't answer the phone when Susan called her own house. "I was really scared and told my work I had an emergency. I drove home crying all the way."

Susan had good reason to worry. Amy had been living with severe depression for at least two years but had refused to see a therapist. "She'd made an attempt on her life the year before using over-the-counter sleeping pills," Susan says. While Amy didn't lose consciousness, emergency room staff determined it had been a real suicide attempt. The hospital transferred Amy to an adolescent psychiatric unit at a regional medical center.

Amy stayed in the psych ward for three months. She had therapy, saw a psychiatrist, and started taking an antidepressant medication. Susan visited every day. She attended family counseling along with Amy's father and her older sister. "Amy continued in therapy after discharge. When we met with the therapist, Amy would hardly say anything. But as soon as we left, she was all smiles and talkative. 'What should we do tonight, Mommy?' It was so frustrating that she couldn't open up to those who could help her."

When Susan pulled into her driveway that January afternoon, she saw a piece of notebook paper taped to the front door. "It was a note to me from Amy—a suicide note. She wanted me to know before I went inside. I ran down the hall and found Amy lying on a couch. I called 911, and it seemed it took only seconds for the paramedics to arrive. They rushed Amy to the hospital without me. I drove myself to the hospital feeling that I'd saved Amy's life by finding her in time. But when I got there, the staff told me that Amy had overdosed on her meds. They hadn't been able to revive her. Amy was dead. I cried hysterically for a while. They let me see my beautiful daughter lying there in the hospital."

In her suicide note, Amy asked Susan to take care of her birds and cat and told her not to cry. "I hate it when you cry." She also wrote, "Mommy, I love you" six times. Susan remembers, "She said she couldn't live for me anymore because she felt like she was dying inside."

LEFT BEHIND

Amy is one of more than forty-one thousand Americans who take their own lives each year. Suicide is the tenth-leading cause of death in the United States, where one person dies by suicide every thirteen minutes. For each suicide, there are at least twenty-five nonfatal suicide attempts. One study showed that more than 10 percent of teen girls and just over 5 percent of teen boys in grades nine through twelve have attempted suicide. According to the Centers for Disease Control and Prevention (CDC), suicide accounts for more years of life lost than any cause

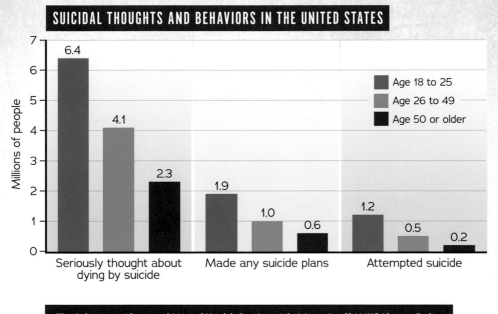

SUICIDAL THOUGHTS AND BEHAVIORS IN THE UNITED STATES

Millions of people

Seriously thought about dying by suicide: Age 18 to 25 — 6.4, Age 26 to 49 — 4.1, Age 50 or older — 2.3

Made any suicide plans: Age 18 to 25 — 1.9, Age 26 to 49 — 1.0, Age 50 or older — 0.6

Attempted suicide: Age 18 to 25 — 1.2, Age 26 to 49 — 0.5, Age 50 or older — 0.2

The Substance Abuse and Mental Health Services Administration (SAMHSA) compiled this data about adults' suicidal thoughts and behaviors over the course of one year (2008-2009).

of death except cancer and heart disease. And suicide is on the rise. Between 2000 and 2013, the annual rate of suicide in the United States has climbed from 10.4 suicide deaths per 100,000 Americans to 12.6 per 100,000 Americans.

Those are just the suicides that coroners—government officials who investigate suicides and other suspicious or unexplained deaths— are certain about. No one is sure how many hundreds or even thousands more people purposefully overdose on drugs, deliberately drive their cars into trees, or take their lives in other ways that cannot be positively confirmed as suicide. These figures also don't account for people who attempt suicide but survive. Nearly half a million Americans were treated in emergency rooms for self-inflicted injuries in the year 2013 alone. Experts estimate that millions more think about suicide but take no action.

SUICIDAL BEHAVIORS

The Centers for Disease Control and Prevention, the Department of Defense, and the Department of Veterans Affairs use shared definitions for different types of suicidal behaviors. Consistent definitions help mental health professionals better assess suicide, identify high-risk groups, and monitor effects of suicide prevention programs. These are the accepted terms and behaviors the three institutions use:

- **Suicidal ideation:** thinking about, considering, or planning suicide
- **Suicide attempt:** a nonfatal, self-directed, potentially injurious behavior with an intent to die as a result of the behavior; might not result in injury
- **Suicide:** death caused by self-directed injurious behavior with the intent to die as a result of the behavior

Americans are not the only people who commit suicide. It is a global issue, accounting for more than half of the world's 1.5 million violent deaths each year. Worldwide, suicide kills more people than war, murder, and natural disaster combined. In 2014 the World Health Organization (WHO) issued its first report on global suicide. The report presents WHO research that calculates that one person dies by suicide every forty seconds, for a total of more than eight hundred thousand people each year. Countries with the highest suicide rates are Guyana, North Korea, South Korea, Sri Lanka, Lithuania, Suriname, Mozambique, Nepal, Tanzania, and Burundi.

SURVIVORS LEFT BEHIND

Sometimes a local newspaper writes a story about a person's suicide or a TV reporter briefly mentions it. Kids at school may talk at their lockers about someone they know who died from suicide. Adults at the workplace talk in the lunchroom. But often those conversations only scratch the surface of the tragedy. Suicide doesn't happen in isolation.

Each suicide affects at least six people—parents, children, siblings, spouses, and good friends—leaving behind nearly five million people who must cope with the long-term fallout of suicide.

The Alliance of Hope for Suicide Survivors, an organization dedicated to helping those coping with a loved one's suicide, says that suicide is like a grenade going off inside a family, leaving people deeply wounded and forever changed. Many friends and family members struggle with devastating emotions, altered relationships, and challenging responsibilities. According to the Alliance of Hope, each situation is unique, but survivors often share the same issues.

> "The event shook my universe, crumbled my stable foundation, and sent shockwaves far into the future."
>
> —David W. Cox, whose father died of suicide when he was nine years old

Shock usually immediately follows the suicide. Shock is a psychological and physical response to an extremely traumatic event. It may cause numbness, confusion, and problems with concentration, making everyday activities difficult or even impossible. For some survivors, shock is worsened by additional trauma related to the suicide. A person may have to launch a frantic search for a missing loved one who is later discovered to have committed suicide. Rescue or resuscitation attempts may have failed. Or a person may have been the one to discover the body of the suicide victim. Shock can last days, weeks, or months and can vary in severity. "Is it normal to feel that you are just existing, no feelings at all, kind of numb?" one survivor asks. "I feel as though I'm still in shock. I don't think it has really hit me yet."

In the wake of losing someone to suicide, many people struggle with *pain and depression*. Common symptoms of grief-triggered depression include insomnia, loss of appetite, lack of energy, and intense sadness. Survivors often say that before the loss they had no idea that emotional pain could be so deep and could hurt so much. Some survivors feel that even mental health professionals cannot understand their pain. "The pain is just overwhelming," confesses one survivor. "At times it takes my breath away and I think, how can I survive? This is just too much to be able to bear." After a loved one's suicide, people may think about committing suicide themselves. For a time, they may not be able to picture a future for themselves without their loved one and may not see any reason to go on living.

Anger is another common and natural response. Friends and family members may feel anger at doctors who prescribed medications that didn't work, anger at therapists whose counseling sessions didn't help enough, or anger at themselves for not recognizing warning signs in a loved one's behavior. "I'm angry that I can't cope with my grief," one survivor says. "I'm angry that everyone's life is going on and mine is not. . . . I'm angry at the people who gave him [my son] the gun. I'm angry they seem to have no sadness or remorse." Anger at the lost loved one can also surface. One survivor of a loved one's suicide says, "When he took his life, I am sure that he did not think for one minute about the consequences of what he was about to do. He would not have thought about how I wake every night with thoughts running through my head about his death, the pain, the anger . . . God, sometimes I feel so angry."

Guilt plagues many suicide survivors. They ask themselves how they missed the warning signs. Or they believe that if they had spent more time with the victim, they could have prevented the suicide. Often people find it easier to blame themselves for the suicide than to blame the suicide victim whom they loved. Some survivors experience relief that their loved one's pain and suffering—mental or physical—has ended. While feelings of relief are natural, they can lead to even more guilt.

Drew, a young man who survived his suicide attempt when he was in the eleventh grade, says, "I would like to get it across to the families and friends of suicide victims that it's not about something they did or didn't do. They need to stop blaming themselves for their loved one's decision to die. It's not about them. It's about the individual." Other supporters of those struggling with guilt echo Drew's sentiments. Overcoming guilt is a difficult but necessary step in the healing process.

Grief has no time limit. Anger and guilt are not on a schedule. Kitty Workman turned ninety-seven years old in 2016. Her son Steuart took his life in 1978 when he was twenty-two years old. "I live it all the time. You can never forget that," she says. "Even now—nearly forty years later—I have a crying jag when I think about it."

Domenica Di Piazza, who lost her mother to suicide, says, "You feel grief for however long you feel it, whether it's one second or the rest of your life. Grief is not something you can predict. It may come on the anniversary of the loved one's birthday or of the suicide itself. It may come when you're crossing the street on your way to work or school. Don't push away your grief. Look it straight in the face, feel it in its many forms, whether it be sorrow or blinding rage. Get help to deal with it."

Recovery may seem to be an impossible goal, yet most survivors eventually move beyond the tragedy and find happiness and meaning in their lives once more. Zelda Williams's father, actor and comedian Robin Williams, took his life in 2014. The following year, Zelda reflected that she had learned to deal with her grief by acknowledging it honestly. "Avoiding fear, sadness, or anger is not the same thing as being happy. I live my sadness every day, but I don't resent it anymore. Instead, I do it now so that the wonderful moments of joy I do find are not in order to forget, but to inhabit and enjoy for their own sake. It's not easy. In fact, I'd say it takes much more effort to consciously do than it does to just stay sad, but with all my heart, I cannot tell you how worth it it is."

> "We never, ever expected this. He seemed fine. He never said "goodbye." He said "good night." He went to bed fully never intending to go to school. . . . I still feel guilty. What if we would have started him on his medication earlier? What if we had noticed something?"
>
> —Pam Cornelius, speaking of her son's suicide at the age of fifteen

If someone you care about loses a loved one to suicide, here are some ways to offer support:

- Volunteer to do something specific, such as helping with grocery shopping, cleaning, or walking the dog.
- Surround your friend with love and understanding but respect his need for private time.
- Let your friend talk about the loss and about her feelings. Be prepared to hear and to accept a wide range of emotions: anger, grief, guilt, sorrow, and deep pain. Don't interrupt. You don't even need to say anything. Just listen and give your friend a safe space in which to reflect, express anger, or cry.
- Help keep track of condolence cards, phone calls, and visitors your friend receives. He'll want that information later.
- Give special attention to other members of the family who may also be grieving. For instance, offer to play with your friend's younger sibling or keep your friend's elderly relative company.
- Know that holidays, birthdays, and anniversaries are likely to be especially difficult times. Your friend will especially need your support and love at these times. Sending a card can be a loving gesture that makes a difference.

LEARNING TO COPE

The American Foundation for Suicide Prevention (AFSP) says that 85 percent of people will lose someone they care about to suicide during their lifetime. Organizations for suicide survivors aim to help survivors and assure them they are not alone. For example, the AFSP suggests reaching out to a support group, which can provide a safe place for those touched by suicide loss. The site offers a state-by-state listing of in-person support groups, as well as specialized online support groups.

"Coping with the suicide of a loved one is a lifelong work in progress," says Domenica Di Piazza. "For a brief period, I was part of a

Support groups can be a valuable resource for people coping with a loved one's suicide. Survivors can share their stories and offer empathy to those in similar situations.

suicide grief group led by grief therapists. The most meaningful part of that experience was hearing other people's stories of the actual suicide of their loved ones. I needed to hear about the ways people took their lives and how they were discovered. I wanted to know how survivors dealt with the aftermath and how they talked to people about suicide. I needed to hear that my story was not strange or unusual and that I was not alone in my experience."

Chris Crutcher, a noted author of young adult fiction, a certified mental health therapist, and a child mental health specialist describes how he offers support to survivors of those who commit suicide. "I would tell survivors to grieve, and I would use my training to get that process started. I would tell them to curse and cry and shake their fists until they felt they didn't need to do it anymore. I would highlight over and over that the suicide was not their fault, that suicide is a decision made by the person who commits it. I would also direct survivors to get involved with service organizations. Feeling helpful improves the chance of balancing out survivors' emotional responses to the death."

As a mental health specialist and an acclaimed young adult fiction author, Chris Crutcher strives to support teens who have suffered losses and who struggle with tragedies beyond their control.

People who feel uncomfortable in a group setting may prefer to consult online groups and forums or to read books and articles about surviving suicide. Others turn to religious or spiritual advisers for guidance. Survivors learn to cope in their own way. Susan Caldwell worked with a support group at a suicide prevention center, as well as a personal grief counselor and a psychiatrist. These experiences "helped immeasurably in my being able to eventually cope with the loss of my daughter," Susan says.

One survivor of a loved one's suicide posted on an online forum: "This forum and the people here told me I was going to survive this, and of course I knew they had to be wrong, but somehow day by day, sometimes hour by hour, I am surviving and you will too." Another said, "It's so empowering to read these posts and realize that we all have things to be proud of, even in the midst of our tragedy and loss."

Suicide can carry a stigma—a perceived mark of shame and disgrace. For this reason, coping with the stigma of a loved one's suicide may pose an unexpected challenge to survivors. If a boyfriend dies in an auto accident, if a sister dies of cancer, or if a parent dies of a heart attack, people are quick to offer emotional support and material help. While accidents and illnesses are widely acknowledged and understood as tragic, unavoidable causes of death, suicide is often frowned upon and is much more difficult to understand.

As a result, people may find news of a suicide baffling or frightening and may not know how to respond. Some people hold strong prejudices against suicide, believing it to be shameful or sinful. They may say the person was selfish and took the easy way out—or even that the person's family is at fault for not loving the person enough. These beliefs stem from an incomplete understanding of the complex and painful issues that lead to suicide. Still, as the veil of secrecy and shame begins to lift through awareness and education, an increasing number of people are gaining an understanding of the forces that drive a person to commit such an extreme and irreversible act.

HEALING AND REBUILDING

Heather Landon was at work when her father called with news that changed her life. "Dad phoned to say that my brother, Jesse, had shot himself in the head. He died instantly." Jesse was thirty years old at the time of his suicide. For years Heather's family had tried to support Jesse as he wrestled with emotional problems and substance abuse. "He'd had a hard life. He had very low self-esteem and few close friends. Jesse got admitted to a drug rehab program when he was sixteen after the police found him drunk and passed out in the snow."

As an adult, Jesse also struggled with physical health issues. "He injured his knee at work and went through several knee surgeries," Heather says. "Being on crutches for years left him with back and neck pain. Living with chronic pain really took a toll on him. He abused his prescription pain medications and took illegal drugs. Our parents took him back into their house when they discovered he was homeless. They tried to help him and insisted that he see a therapist. But after a few weeks, our parents discovered he was lying and stealing money from them. They asked him to leave."

SUICIDE AND RELIGION

Some of those left behind by a loved one's suicide may feel stranded by their religious beliefs. Traditionally, many faiths teach that suicide is a sin, contributing to a stigma surrounding the deed. Religious families may experience shame if they believe their faith blames their loved one for the suicide. Traditional religious views of suicide include the following:

- *Christianity.* The Bible mentions but does not condemn suicide. However, in the fifth century CE, Christian philosopher Saint Augustine declared suicide to be such a terrible sin that it would keep a person's soul from going to heaven. In Catholicism, suicide has traditionally been considered a mortal sin, meaning that a person who commits suicide will go to hell. Most Protestant denominations of Christianity traditionally teach that suicide goes against God's will and is morally wrong.
- *Islam.* Only God determines when a person leaves this world. Suicide is considered to be a great sin.
- *Judaism.* Suicide is considered a very grave crime.

These traditional views are changing, however. For example, Catholics who take their own lives are no longer denied a Catholic funeral or burial in a Catholic cemetery. Religious leaders of all faiths are more likely to consider the role of mental illness in many suicides, believing that people who commit suicide are not fully responsible for their actions.

Religious leaders expressed a range of views regarding suicide and religion in a 2005 interview for PBS:

Father Charles Rubey said that since the 1980s, "the [Catholic] Church has looked more benignly on survivors and on people who have taken their lives. They [Catholic leaders] took the whole issue of suicide out of the moral realm and placed it in the medical realm where it belongs."

Rabbi Joseph Ozarowski focused on how Judaism can support those left behind after a suicide. "We have an especial obligation to offer comfort to the family because of the societal stigma associated with a suicide and because the survivors themselves are probably sharing some guilt or having some very deep emotional feelings."

Imam Inamul Haq noted that in cases of severe mental illness, Islam can make allowances for those who commit suicide. "A person who is normal, healthy, rational [and] balanced will not commit suicide. If I did not choose something with clear intention, Islamically I'm not liable for that act."

The Reverend Jerry Andrews, a Presbyterian pastor, summed up his perspective as a Protestant Christian: "All human sin is forgiven. God's nature is merciful. It is everlasting."

Jesse's suicide plunged the Landon family into despair. "Both my parents attempted suicide after Jesse's death. Mom overdosed with a combination of prescription and over-the-counter medications. The stress of dealing with Jesse's death and Mom's suicide attempt was too much for my dad. He shot himself in the stomach. He lived, but his injuries were severe."

Heather recalls, "After Jesse's death, I heard his voice in my dreams every night. I wrote this poem a week after he died.

Now that your life has ended by your own hand,

No truth revealed,

Demons lay silent, no voice to sing out.

Loved ones remain, lost and broken-hearted.

Blame, guarded and sheltered, in need of answers.

Why?"

Gradually, however, Heather found a way to move forward. "I started taking a look at my loved ones after this and realized they could be gone at any moment," she says, reflecting on the lessons she drew from her brother's tragic loss. "You can't wait for a holiday or special occasion to tell someone how you feel. You have to show them every day how much they mean to you. You may never get another chance! I struggle every day with the loss and depression that plagues my family. I try to shield my children from the sorrow that I've been through. I try to stay positive and loving. I still cry over my brother's death and my parents' suicide attempts, but every day I try to make it better for me and my family."

BY THE NUMBERS

- An estimated 4.9 million people in the United States have lost loved ones to suicide.
- Worldwide, at least 800,000 people die from suicide each year.
- An American dies by suicide every thirteen minutes.
- Suicide is the tenth-leading cause of death in the United States.

Chapter 2

RISK FACTORS FOR SUICIDE

An ambulance with its siren blaring pulled to a stop below Jeanne Miller's fifth-floor office at the Lawrence Berkeley National Laboratory in Berkeley, California. "After hearing more sirens over the next few minutes, I joined a small crowd on the balcony," Jeanne says. "Below us was a stretcher with a body covered by a sheet. A coworker said someone had jumped to his death from the floor above us. We didn't know until the next morning that it was Mike."

On that muggy afternoon in October 2006, with the sun hanging low in the sky, world-famous physicist Michael Ronan climbed onto a chair on the sixth-floor balcony at Berkeley Lab and jumped to his death. Earlier that day, Professor Ronan had met with his physics students at the University of California, Berkeley. He told the class he was too depressed to continue teaching and said good-bye to them.

Jeanne Miller knew Dr. Ronan for thirty years. "Everyone liked Mike. He was friendly and funny and full of energy. I never saw him any other way. Everybody I talked to was stunned. It was a lost day. We could barely function. In the afternoon, there was a meeting in the auditorium with grief counselors present. People tried to understand how his life had come to this. During the next few days, people were especially kind to one another."

"His closest friends and family knew about his depression, but he kept it from most of the people he worked with," Jeanne says. "At the memorial service, there were email tributes from colleagues and heads of physics laboratories in the United States and Europe. It was clear the physics world had lost a talented, creative, and much-loved scientist."

Jeanne thinks of Mike whenever she hears about a suicide, even after so much time has passed. "I learned that on the afternoon Mike ended his life, he had reached out for help. He made plans to have dinner with a close friend, arranged to spend the night with another friend, and made an appointment with his therapist for the next morning. These were caring people who offered him comfort and support. But that wasn't enough. He made a dash to the balcony minutes after his last call. To me that speaks of the anguish depression brings. He couldn't bear another hour of the pain."

> These were caring people who offered him comfort and support. But that wasn't enough. . . . To me that speaks of the anguish depression brings.
>
> —Jeanne Miller

WHO COMMITS SUICIDE?

Good friends and a rewarding career were not enough to keep Dr. Ronan from ending his life. His situation is not unique. Over the past decade, the number of people who die from suicide in the United States has grown faster than can be expected from population growth alone. What can explain this? According to WHO's 2014 report on suicide, "There is no single explanation of why people die by suicide." While each person is unique and responds differently to stressors, mental health professionals have identified several common risk factors for suicide, including mental illness and substance abuse. The more risk factors that are present, the higher the risk for suicide, even if the risk is not immediate.

- *Access to lethal means.* People are more likely to commit suicide if they have tools that allow them to harm themselves. Access to guns, knives, or prescription drugs (including sedatives, sleeping pills, and narcotics) greatly increases the risk that people may take their lives. As the WHO report notes, "However, many suicides happen impulsively and, in such circumstances, easy access to a means of suicide . . . can make the difference as to whether a person lives or dies."

- *Difficulty gaining access to health care.* Finding and affording treatment for physical and mental health problems is difficult for many people. Margaret Chan, WHO's director-general, notes that even for those who do seek treatment, "Many health systems and services fail to provide timely and effective help."

- *Stressors such as disaster, war, trauma, and isolation.* Circumstances largely beyond an individual's control can create severe strain that may lead to suicidal behavior.

- *Individual factors such as mental illness, substance abuse, or physical health problems.* When people are in great physical or mental distress due to individual emotional and physical struggles, the risk for suicide rises. Mental illness and substance abuse are the strongest individual risk factors for suicide. While 90 percent of people with such conditions do *not* take their own lives, at least nine out of ten people who die from suicide are struggling with mental illness or substance abuse.

Other individual risk factors include genetics; family and domestic violence; bullying; being gay, lesbian, bisexual, or transgender; major life losses; a family history of suicide; and previous suicide attempts. Suicide is not confined to any age, gender, ethnic background, or economic group. Anyone can be at risk for suicide. However, a person's gender, age, and background can affect the likelihood that the person will take his or her life.

For example, suicide is four times higher among males than among females. While more women than men try to take their lives, men are more likely to complete the act, largely because males and females tend to attempt suicide in different ways. More than half of suicides among males occur by guns and many others occur by hanging, both of which are highly lethal methods. The greatest number of completed and attempted suicides among females occurs by poisoning (involving both illegal drugs and prescription medications). Suicide attempts involving these substances are less likely to result in death because people may ingest a nonlethal dosage or may be saved by swift medical intervention.

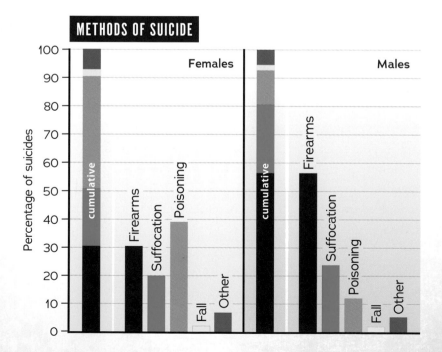

Men may also have risk factors that women typically don't. "Men are much less likely to seek help than women are," says psychologist Michelle Cornette, executive director of the American Association of Suicidology. She notes that many women seek support and comfort from female friends when they have serious problems. "[Men] utilize their friendships in different ways. Men are less likely to disclose to a male friend that they are struggling psychologically." Men may turn inward and try to handle their problems by themselves at the very time they most need help.

ETHNICITY AND AGE

The highest rates of suicides in the United States are among American Indians and Alaska Natives, followed by Caucasians. Suicide rates for Asian and Pacific Islanders, African Americans, and Hispanics are about one-third as high as Caucasians. Researchers cannot be certain why some groups appear more vulnerable than others, but certain risk factors may be more prevalent among certain groups. For example, American Indians and Alaska Natives tend to experience high rates of poverty, limited access to education and health care, and high unemployment. Groups with lower suicide rates may experience stronger protective factors, such as close family ties and religious affiliation, believed to result in fewer suicides. Christine Moutier, chief medical officer for the American Foundation for Suicide Prevention, says lower rates of suicide for African Americans are generally attributed to strong traditions of family support, robust social networks, and religious faith.

However, a study published in 2015 reported that the suicide rate among African American children between the ages of five and eleven has doubled since 1993. "I was shocked," says Dr. Jeffrey Bridge, who led the study. "I'll be honest with you. I looked at it [the data] and I thought, 'Did we do the analysis correctly?' I thought we had made a mistake." Researchers theorized that the trend might be related to lower average ages of puberty for black children. Black children in the United States are also statistically more likely to be exposed to violence and traumatic stress than children of other ethnic groups.

The prevalence of suicide also varies by age. Children under the age of fifteen have the lowest rate of suicide, followed by young people between the ages of fifteen and twenty-four—although teens may be especially vulnerable to suicidal thoughts at this point in their lives. The highest suicide rate is found in people forty-five to sixty-four years old.

Teens often struggle with a variety of stressors that can put them at risk for suicide.

The second-highest rate is among those who are eighty-five years and older. Stress, problems with money and jobs, and legal issues are likely to be contributing factors to suicide in the middle-age group, while painful or terminal illness and unrecognized depression are likely to be contributing factors among the oldest.

JOINER'S THEORY OF SUICIDE

Psychologist Thomas E. Joiner Jr. was twenty-five years old when his father died from suicide. Because of his father's death, Joiner focused his life's work on suicide. He studied suicide for decades and talked to patients for hundreds of hours.

Joiner developed a seven-word answer to the question: Why do people die by suicide? "Because they want to. Because they can," he told *Newsweek* writer Tony Dokoupil during an interview. "People will die by suicide when they have both the desire to die and the ability to die."

Yet many of the risk factors that drive people to suicide are also common conditions or experiences that most people endure without becoming suicidal. Many people feel alone at times; have problems making or keeping friends; lack family support; or live with illness and pain, which may make them feel they are a burden to others. However, when one of these factors persists for a long period of time or reaches an unbearable level, people may begin to wrestle with thoughts of suicide. The struggle can intensify if someone is dealing with more than one of these factors at the same time. When a person is dealing with one or more risk factors and has the means (such as pills or guns) of inflicting self-harm, the risk for suicide becomes very high.

Based on his research, Joiner shaped his "interpersonal theory of suicide." He believes the pathway to suicide is through a set of overlapping conditions that can be shown on a Venn diagram. The exact combination of factors that could push someone to commit suicide is different for each person, but the two constants are the desire to end one's life and the means to do so. When the conditions overlap, they create a dark area where escape is difficult. For instance, when people feel lonely or isolated and they believe they have become a burden to others and they have the desire to end their lives and they have the means to do so, they begin to see suicide as a real possibility.

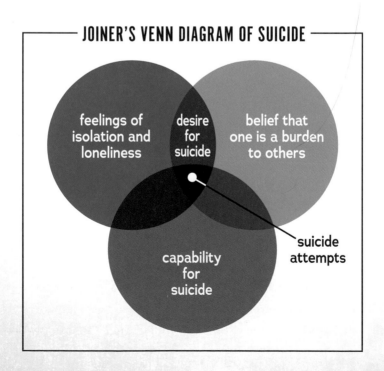

JOINER'S VENN DIAGRAM OF SUICIDE

feelings of isolation and loneliness

desire for suicide

belief that one is a burden to others

capability for suicide

suicide attempts

"A HOWLING TEMPEST IN THE BRAIN"

Mental illnesses that can increase the risk of suicide include mood disorders (such as depression and bipolar disorder), anxiety disorders (extreme anxiety and unfounded fears), paranoia (extreme distrust and suspicion of others), and schizophrenia. Of these, depression is among the most common. In his 1990 memoir, *Darkness Visible: A Memoir of Madness*, American novelist William Styron described depression as a "howling tempest in the brain." At one point, Styron experienced severe depression and seriously thought about suicide. He lost all sense of joy in life and suffered exhaustion, feelings of worthlessness, and a loss of self-esteem.

"The pain is unrelenting," Styron wrote. "In virtually any other serious sickness, a patient who felt similar devastation would be lying flat in bed, possibly sedated and hooked up to the tubes and wires of life support systems. The sufferer from depression has no such option and therefore finds himself, like a walking casualty of war, thrust into intolerable social and family situations."

Nearly everyone has experienced some degree of depression for short periods of time. Breaking up with a boyfriend or girlfriend, losing an important competition, arguing with a family member, grieving the death of a loved one, and other upsetting events can lead to periods of intense sadness. Yet in these situations, most of us don't think about taking our own lives. After some time passes, most people come to terms with painful experiences and find ways to move on. The depression that follows a sad event, such as a death in the family or the loss of a job, tends to lessen and even to disappear. It usually does not affect people's daily activities longer than a few weeks or months.

By contrast, a severe and persistent depression may not be linked to any particular event or circumstance and can last indefinitely. The more severe form of depression is called major depression, or clinical depression. One report by the Substance Abuse and Mental Health Services Administration found that nearly 11 percent of adolescents in the United States had experienced an episode of major depression in the previous year.

According to the Mayo Clinic, a person must have five or more symptoms that last most of the day, nearly every day, over a two-week period for a doctor to make a diagnosis of major depression. These are the symptoms:

- Feelings of sadness or emptiness, often involving frequent urges to cry, may appear as irritability in children and teens
- Reduced interest or pleasure in normal activities
- Significantly decreased or increased appetite, often accompanied by weight loss or weight gain
- Insomnia or an increased desire to sleep
- Changes in behavior that other people notice
- Low energy

- Feelings of worthlessness or guilt
- Problems with thinking, concentrating, and making decisions
- Thinking about death or suicide, or actually attempting suicide

THE ABSENCE OF HOPE

Libba Bray, a widely known, award-winning author of young adult novels, wrote a blog entry in 2014 titled, "Miles and Miles of No-Man's Land," about living with severe depression. "Depression isn't like being sad or blue or wistful," she said. "It is crippling. It is a constant whine in your head, making it hard to hear yourself think. . . . In this state, you can only think of how desperately you want this agony to end. You can only think of doing something, anything, to stop the feeling, to keep it from overwhelming you with shame, loneliness, guilt, and bleak-gray hopelessness. This is what it is to experience depression. It is the absence of hope."

A related mental illness, bipolar disorder, can also be associated with an increased risk of suicide. People with bipolar disorder experience wide mood swings ranging from deep depression to extreme highs called manic episodes. During a manic episode, people are euphoric, overactive, highly excited, and sometimes delusional. During periods of deep depression, people with bipolar disorder feel sadness, hopelessness, and loss of interest in activities. Between 25 and 50 percent of people with bipolar disorder attempt suicide at some point in their lives.

> "The best way that I can describe my depression is that my brain hates who I am. Either through bad wiring or misfiring neurons, it hates me."
>
> —Gordon, a college student who tried to take his life

Michelle Prichard has lived with bipolar disorder since she was a teenager. A few years ago, when she was in her early twenties, an innocent conversation with friends triggered her worst episode of depression and suicidal thinking. "My friends appeared to have everything together, and to have reached major life achievements," Michelle says. "It made me feel small and worthless, and held down by my disorder, even though they weren't comparing my life to theirs at all."

She goes on, "The feeling of being so insignificant made me want to end my life because I felt that I would never measure up to others. I had several ideas of how I could do that. My family stripped the house of anything I could use to harm myself—knives, razor blades, pills. It was a difficult, debilitating period. Time felt slow, sluggish, and dark." Michelle is stable and doing better every day, she says.

Kevin Hines, one of the few people to survive a jump off San Francisco's Golden Gate Bridge, has also struggled with bipolar disorder. He was only nineteen years old when he jumped, but he says he didn't want to die. "It was not my rational, conscious choice or decision. I believed I *had* to [die]. Compelled by my bipolar disorder, my brain illness, I was to complete this terrible act." Kevin climbed over the bridge railing and fell the equivalent of twenty-five stories into the sea, shattering part of his spine and damaging internal organs. After Hines recovered from his severe injuries, he wrote a memoir called *Cracked, Not Broken: Surviving and Thriving after a Suicide Attempt*, published in 2013. After years of treatment for his mental illness, he became a powerful advocate and speaker for suicide prevention.

THE MYSTERIOUS CAUSES OF DEPRESSION

For decades scientists have believed that a chemical imbalance in the brain causes depression. Doctors may treat depressed patients with a mix of antianxiety drugs, mood stabilizers, antidepressants, and antipsychotics. These medications affect natural chemicals in the brain called neurotransmitters. The brain uses neurotransmitters to send signals between neurons—cells that transmit nerve impulses. When

IN SAD CAGES

Health-care workers in some emergency rooms are trained to use the mnemonic "In SAD CAGES" to screen patients who seem depressed. Depending on how patients answer the questions, they may be hospitalized for observation and treatment or referred to a counselor or psychiatrist.

In Interest. Have you lost interest in activities you normally enjoy or care about?

S Sleep. Has there been any change in your sleep pattern? Are you sleeping more or less?

A Appetite. Is there a change in your appetite? Are you eating more or less?

D Depression. Are you feeling consistently unhappy?

C Concentration. Are you having difficulty focusing on tasks or conversations?

A Activity. Is there a change in your physical or social activity level? Are you participating in fewer activities than usual or showing less interest in activities?

G Guilt. Are you feeling guilty about anything?

E Energy. Is there a change in your energy level?

S Suicide. Are you thinking about suicide or planning to take your life?

a neurotransmitter moves from one neuron to the next, it stimulates the neuron or slows it. A person's behavior may change depending on which neurons the medication affects.

Doctors believe the neurotransmitters dopamine, norepinephrine, and serotonin greatly influence behavior, mood, attention, and other brain functions. A low level of serotonin in the brain is thought to be a key trigger of depression, and for that reason, many antidepressants increase the amount of serotonin in the brain. Yet one-third of people treated with antidepressants see no change in their condition, while many others feel a little better but are still depressed.

Psychology professors Hal Arkowitz and Scott Lilienfeld, writing for *Scientific American* in 2014, asked, "If antidepressants correct a chemical imbalance that underlies depression, all or most depressed people should get better after taking them. That they do not suggests that we have only barely begun to understand the disorder at a molecular level." In other words, a shortage of certain neurotransmitters may not cause depression after all—even though boosting the level of those neurotransmitters in the brain can be an effective treatment for some people with depression. As Arkowitz and Lilienfeld point out, "Aspirin alleviates headaches, but headaches are not caused by a deficiency of aspirin."

Joseph Coyle, professor of neuroscience at Harvard Medical School, agrees that focusing on neurotransmitters may not provide a complete picture of the causes and triggers of depression. "Chemical imbalance is sort of last-century thinking. [Depression is] much more complicated than that," he noted in 2012. While antidepressant medications that raise serotonin levels will likely remain a treatment option for a long time, researchers still aren't certain what causes depression or, in many cases, how to relieve suffering.

Some studies show that certain parts of the brain that deal with emotion and impulse control are smaller and less active in depressed people. This has led some researchers to speculate that structural abnormalities in the brain can contribute to depression. Factors such as genetics, the environment, and stress may also play a role in depression and mental illness, and further research will likely uncover other factors at play.

SUBSTANCE ABUSE

One in three people who die by suicide are under the influence of alcohol or drugs at the time of death. Suicide can be closely linked to substance abuse—the misuse of potentially harmful substances, including alcohol, illegal drugs, and nonmedical use of certain prescription medications, such as pain medications and sedatives. People use drugs and alcohol to produce pleasure, relieve stress, reduce physical or emotional pain, and alter their perception of reality. As Carolyn Ross notes in a 2014 *Psychology Today* article, "Many people abuse drugs or alcohol in an attempt to relieve the symptoms of depression, anxiety, or other mental health conditions. The rate of major depression is two to four times higher among addicts than the general population."

Substance abuse is widespread in the United States. A 2013 study estimated that 5.2 percent of adolescents aged twelve to seventeen, as well as an estimated 8.5 percent of adults aged eighteen and older, abuse

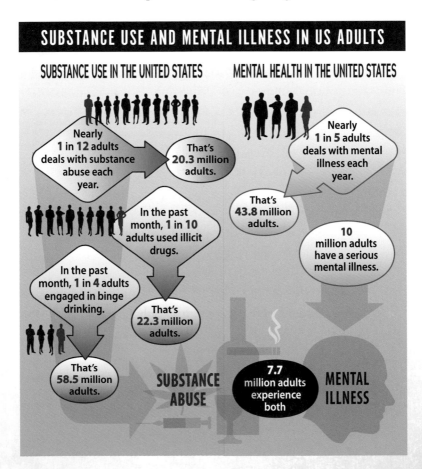

SUBSTANCE USE AND MENTAL ILLNESS IN US ADULTS

SUBSTANCE USE IN THE UNITED STATES

Nearly 1 in 12 adults deals with substance abuse each year.

That's 20.3 million adults.

In the past month, 1 in 10 adults used illicit drugs.

In the past month, 1 in 4 adults engaged in binge drinking.

That's 22.3 million adults.

That's 58.5 million adults.

MENTAL HEALTH IN THE UNITED STATES

Nearly 1 in 5 adults deals with mental illness each year.

That's 43.8 million adults.

10 million adults have a serious mental illness.

SUBSTANCE ABUSE

7.7 million adults experience both

MENTAL ILLNESS

substances. While substance abuse is not the same as addiction, many people who abuse substances do become addicted to them. Addiction occurs when people can no longer control their impulse to use drugs. Changes in brain functioning, especially in the brain's natural inhibition and reward centers, accompany this dependence on drugs. Signs of substance abuse include a strong desire for a drug, difficulties in controlling its use, failure to meet obligations or engage in other usual activities, and continuing to use the drug even if its use causes problems with relationships, accidents, or even arrests.

Ross describes the connection between suicide and substance abuse. "Under the influence of drugs or alcohol, people may lose inhibitions and take risks they ordinarily would not." Yet people who use drugs to cope with mental illness such as depression may find that the drug use actually worsens their condition. "Although drugs may seem to help in the short term, they exacerbate problems over time," Ross notes. In addition, people can face increased suicide risk if they try to stop their drug use without medical supervision. "When attempting to stop using drugs, people may feel overwhelmed by the return of painful emotions that they had been medicating with drugs. They may also be clear-headed enough to carry out suicidal thoughts and plans," says Ross.

The Substance Abuse and Mental Health Services Administration, an agency of the US Department of Health and Human Services, reported these connections between substance abuse and suicide:

- Suicide is the leading cause of death among people who struggle with substance abuse.
- When substance abuse is combined with a mental health issue, the risk of suicide increases even more.
- People treated for alcohol abuse are ten times more at risk for suicide than the general population.
- Alcohol is involved in about 30 to 40 percent of suicides and attempted suicides.

PERSONAL AND FAMILY RISK FACTORS

Factors beyond a person's control can lead to thoughts of suicide and suicide attempts. Major life setbacks, such as the loss of an important relationship or a job, may lead to suicidal thoughts or suicide attempts even in the absence of other risk factors. A serious medical illness may trigger thoughts of suicide, especially among older people. Feelings of hopelessness or isolation, regardless of the reason or the person's age, are linked to a higher risk of suicide.

Lesbian, gay, bisexual, transgender, and queer/questioning (LGBTQ) individuals are at higher risk for suicide than their straight counterparts. Gay men are six times more likely than heterosexual males to attempt suicide, while lesbians are twice as likely as heterosexual females to attempt to kill themselves. The National Transgender Discrimination Survey of 2014 found that 41 percent of transgender and gender-nonconforming respondents reported attempting suicide at some point in their lives. Members of the LGBTQ community often face homophobia and transphobia in many forms, including harassment, bullying, and violence. They may experience self-esteem issues, isolation, and loneliness, which can lead to thoughts of suicide and suicide attempts.

> Gay men are six times more likely than heterosexual males to attempt suicide, while lesbians are twice as likely as heterosexual females to attempt to kill themselves.

Domestic violence is another known trigger for suicide. The vast majority of victims of domestic violence are women and children. One in three women in the United States will be a victim of domestic violence at some point in her life. These emotional and physical attacks leave people feeling trapped, hopeless, and confused. Some blame themselves for the violence inflicted on them. More than a quarter of all women who attempt suicide have experienced domestic violence. Many children who grow up in an abusive family environment attempt suicide.

Author, filmmaker, and youth activist e.E. Charlton-Trujillo recalls the trauma of family abuse during her childhood. "I came from a tough home," she says. "I was an adopted Mexican-American girl in an extended family of mostly racists. At school, I was the kid who stood up for those who were bullied. But at home, my father bullied me to the edges of the imagination. He called me names. He pushed and punched me. He belittled my creativity and thirst for writing. There were times that his cruelty made me want to act out to make other kids feel as small as I did. But something in me held on to the notion that maybe I could do better or be better." For others, the uphill battle against physical and emotional abuse is less successful.

Family members of someone who has committed suicide are more likely to take their own lives. A loved one's suicide may result in depression that in turn leads to a suicide attempt—as was the case with Heather Landon's parents, who both attempted suicide after they lost their son to suicide. Multiple suicides in a family may also reflect shared risk factors for suicide, such as domestic abuse or genetically inherited health problems. Two of Kitty Workman's three children died by suicide. "My children all lived with depression," she says. "We didn't know much about it in those days, but I think it came from their father. His brother—the children's favorite uncle—killed himself as well. This makes me believe suicide runs in families."

Media coverage of suicide by a well-known public figure or of a local suicide may also increase the risk for vulnerable individuals. Approximately 1 percent of all suicides in the United States are associated with other suicides—a process called contagion or copycat suicide. Responsible media reporting can help minimize this by not sensationalizing suicide, by avoiding the terms "successful suicide" and "failed attempt," and by including crisis hotline phone numbers in every suicide-related article or broadcast.

THE ROLE OF GENETICS

In 2013 investigators published a study that found a genetic link to some mental illnesses. The researchers, working in nineteen countries, studied deoxyribonucleic acid (DNA), the molecule that codes for genetic traits, from thirty-three thousand people who had been diagnosed with major depression, bipolar disorder, schizophrenia, and attention deficit/hyperactivity disorder, among other mental illnesses. The first three disorders are known to be associated with family history. Researchers compared the DNA of these subjects with the DNA of twenty-eight thousand people with no known mental disorders.

The study found several genes shared by people with the mental disorders that were not present in those with normal mental health. Two of the genes help control the movement of calcium in and out of brain cells. (Calcium affects the way brain cells communicate.) Depending on other genes and environmental factors, the presence of these genes could contribute to mental illness and suicidal behavior.

In 2014 researchers at the Johns Hopkins University School of Medicine in Baltimore, Maryland, published a paper suggesting an even more direct link between genetics and suicide. The study focused on a mutation (a change in structure) in the SKA2 gene, which affects how people respond to stress hormones. The gene can also change the body's production of certain chemicals. Researchers found that this gene mutation—and the related abnormal levels of specific chemicals in the body—were far more common in people who attempted or committed suicide than in those who had not. While this discovery does not confirm the existence of a genetic trigger for suicide, it does offer a possible way to find out whether people are at risk for suicide. Based on blood tests, which show test subjects' levels of SKA2-linked chemicals, researchers identified people who had attempted suicide with 96 percent accuracy.

"We have found a gene that could be really important for consistently identifying a range of behaviors from suicidal thoughts to [suicide] completion," Zachary Kaminsky, PhD and assistant professor of psychiatry at Johns Hopkins said. "We believe we might be able to monitor the blood to identify those at risk of suicide." Confirmation of the genetic link to mental illness and suicidal tendencies may pave the way for new methods of identifying and treating people at risk for suicide.

UNDERSTANDING RISK AND PROTECTIVE FACTORS

Risk factors do not cause suicide attempts, nor do they determine who will actually take their own lives. Rather, risk factors are traits or conditions that increase the chance that suicide might happen. They make it more likely that a particular person will think about suicide or attempt it. For example, obesity and inactivity are risk factors for a heart attack. However, a person who is obese or who doesn't exercise is not guaranteed to have a heart attack. Recognizing risk factors helps people understand what needs to change in order to decrease a risk over time.

Just as important as risk factors are protective factors, conditions that reduce suicide attempts. Protective factors help people avoid or cope with suicidal thoughts and behavior. One of the most effective protective factors is family and community support—feeling connected to other people. Religious beliefs also protect some people from suicide. Access to effective care for mental health problems, substance abuse disorders, and physical conditions is crucial. Skills in problem solving, conflict resolution, and managing disputes also help to protect people from suicidal thoughts and actions by helping them deal constructively with difficult situations.

BY THE NUMBERS

- Nine out of ten Americans who die by suicide have a substance abuse or mental health disorder.
- An estimated 1.3 million (5.2 percent) of adolescent Americans aged twelve to seventeen have engaged in substance abuse in the past year.
- People who abuse alcohol have a ten times greater risk for suicide than the general population.

For every teen who dies by suicide, at least twenty-five teens attempt it.

Chapter 3

SUICIDE IN CHILDREN AND TEENS

Carlie Madison was ten years old the first time she felt depressed. "But I didn't have suicidal thoughts or cut until I was fourteen," she says. "I don't know exactly why I was depressed, but it runs in my family. My suicidal thoughts scared me, so I talked to my mom." Carlie's mom was deeply upset and worried, so Carlie pretended to feel better. "I perfected the art of not upsetting people."

Carlie found that cutting—using a sharp object to deliberately cut herself—eased her suicidal thoughts. "When I got too emotional about something like an argument with my parents, a break-up with a boyfriend, or just those terrible negative thoughts swirling around in my head, cutting acted as a focal point and a release. It was as if there was a hurricane of horrible thoughts in my head and cutting was the only way to make it stop."

Few people realized Carlie was depressed or that she was cutting, because it didn't interfere with her life. "I went out with friends. I was active in my church and got great grades. The universities I applied to accepted me. Even so, my inner life was full of insecurity and sadness and confusion."

Carlie felt worse when she went to college, but she was reluctant to take medication. "I worried it would change my personality or prevent me from feeling the glorious highs that always seemed to follow my lows. I finally saw a psychiatrist who put me on a small dose of an antidepressant. It really helped to even out my moods. Best of all, *I was still myself.* A few years later, I went off the medication when I wanted to have a baby. Someday I might need to take an antidepressant again and I'm okay with that."

Carlie says, "Even though it's been years since I cut myself, it's still an impulse when my anger and sadness are too much to handle. I feel shame and guilt that I did this to myself. Sometimes I fear my depression and failure to cope will be passed on to my children. I rarely have suicidal thoughts anymore. Now I understand myself better. I know more about depression. I know when and how to reach out for help. Now I realize there are better ways to cope with strong emotions, and I'm still learning about that."

SUICIDE RISKS IN TEENS

As one of thousands of teens who grapple with thoughts of suicide, Carlie had to work hard to overcome her depression and suicidal thoughts. According to a 2014 CDC report about teens and suicide, these are the percentage of students in grades nine through twelve who were depressed or had suicidal behavior during the previous year:

BEHAVIOR	GIRLS	BOYS
Felt sad and hopeless	39.1%	20.8%
Seriously considered suicide	22.4%	11.6%
Made a suicide plan	16.9%	10.3%
Attempted suicide	10.6%	5.4%

For every teen who dies by suicide, at least twenty-five teens attempt it. While suicide is the tenth-leading cause of death nationwide, it's the second-leading cause of death—after accidents—for young people between the ages of ten and twenty-four. Suicide in this age group accounts for about five thousand lives lost each year in the United States, with the most common methods being firearms, suffocation (which includes hanging), and poisoning (which includes overdoses of illegal drugs and prescription medications).

Look around your classroom. Maybe it's a big class with thirty people. Statistically, of those people, eight are feeling sad and hopeless, five are thinking about suicide, and two or three of them have tried it. Look at the girls in your class. They attempt suicide about twice as often as boys. Look at the boys. They are four times more likely to die from suicide than girls. About eight out of ten teens who die from suicide are boys. Teens face many of the same risk factors for suicide that adults do. However, certain risk factors may make suicide more likely for some teens. These include the following:

- Family history. This includes a family history of suicide, mental disorders, and/or substance abuse.
- Personal substance abuse. The use of legal or illegal drugs, alcohol, and other mind-altering substances can create feelings of dependency, illness, and depression. Feeling out of control and powerless due to addiction is a major risk factor in attempted teen suicide.
- Abuse and violence. Abuse—mental, emotional, physical, or sexual—can increase the likelihood of attempted suicide.
- Strong emotions. People may struggle with anxiety, stress, and feelings of hopelessness or worthlessness at any age. Many teens have not yet developed strategies for coping with such emotions and the severe depression that can accompany them.

- Easy access to lethal methods of suicide, especially guns, increases the risk for suicide.
- Lack of a support network, poor relationships with parents or peers, and feelings of social isolation may lead to suicidal thoughts or actions.
- A bisexual or homosexual teen in an unsupportive family or a hostile school environment has a greater risk of suicide than straight teens.
- Bullying—physical or emotional abuse from peers, whether in person or via social media—is a risk factor for teen suicide.

For many teens, suicidal impulses have their roots in multiple factors. When transgender teen Zander (born Sandra Nicole) Mahaffey took his life by suicide in February 2015, he left a lengthy suicide note on his Tumblr blog. "I am a boy," he said, "even if the [world] doesn't see me as one." In addition to feeling that he wasn't accepted for who he was, Zander described enduring physical and emotional abuse from family members and family friends, as well as at least one instance of sexual abuse. Ultimately, he felt overwhelmed by these difficult circumstances. "I'm just so tired, I'm so tired and I just want to go to sleep." After Zander's death, thousands of teens posted his suicide note on social media, hoping that Zander's story would remind other struggling teens, especially transgender teens, that they were not alone.

"Suicide is a complex phenomenon because given the perfect storm of circumstances, one may make a snap-decision that is driven in the moment, whereas other individuals may have planned, or ideated about suicide for years."

—Amanda Lipp, mental health consultant

Mental health advocate Darrell Steinberg, former President pro Tempore of the California State Senate, stands with artist and mental health advocate Amanda Lipp at the 7th annual International Together Against Stigma Conference in February 2015.

Amanda Lipp, who attempted suicide as a teen, struggled with depression as well as a number of other issues that pushed her to desperation. "It was a culmination of a lot of stressors, and my mind couldn't meet its own demands. I was grappling with my sexual identity, family issues, and transitioning into a new school." After her suicide attempt, she was able to get more effective help in dealing with these issues. "It wasn't until I hit rock bottom and almost took my own life that I realized I had something to live for."

CUTTING: A WARNING SIGN

Cutting is a form of self-harm involving the use of razors or other sharp objects to inflict a cut, usually on a part of the body that can be easily concealed by clothing. People who cut, especially teens, use cutting to distract themselves from emotional pain, to help maintain control over the environment, to manage guilt or self-hatred, or as a form of self-punishment. Overall, about 1 percent of the US population has engaged in self-harm at some point. Between 13 and 24 percent of high school students in the United States and Canada admit to self-harm, with girls doing it more often than boys. Cutting is generally a symptom of a larger problem, such as depression, and can indicate a risk for suicide. While more than half of the people who admit to cutting say they do not have suicidal thoughts, cutting and suicidal ideation are connected. One study showed that about 8 percent of people who cut had made a suicide attempt in the past. The problems that drive a person to inflict self-harm can intensify over time, escalating a person's distress and leading to thoughts of more drastic measures, including suicidal ideation.

Warning signs that someone may be cutting or engaging in another form of self-harm include the following:

- Wearing baggy clothing or wearing long sleeves on warm days
- Having visible cuts and wounds on the body
- Spending long periods locked in a bedroom or bathroom
- Leaving razors, scissors, and knives in unexpected places

In most cases, people cut *instead* of attempting suicide. Rather than wishing to end their lives, they hope to alleviate their suffering in a nonlethal way. Carlie Madison used cutting to cope with her depression and anxiety. So did Davis Evans, a twenty-four-year-old food service worker living in New Mexico. He began cutting when he was twenty years old. "I had just left a psychology class that included an extremely casual and not to be taken seriously intelligence test, which I bombed," he said. "It seemed to me that I ought to punish myself for my shortcoming. Cutting started out as a punishment, but over time it mutated into a habit, a distraction from stress. I had gotten so used to it that the cutting genuinely felt good, like taking a shower that was right on the edge of too hot."

Davis had been dealing with suicidal thoughts long before he started cutting. "One day I tied the end of a bathrobe belt around my neck and tied the other end to a hook on a door. I don't really think

TIPS FOR DEPRESSED TEENS

Clinical depression is a serious mental health concern that requires medical intervention. Experts advise those who suffer from depression to seek professional help. Family doctors can help make recommendations for therapists, as can a school counselor. Other strategies for coping with depression, along with talk therapy and medication as prescribed by a doctor, include the following:

- Try not to isolate yourself. Spend time with friends and family, even if it seems difficult. Being with others and doing things you used to enjoy can make you feel better.
- Keep your body healthy. Eat well and exercise. An unhealthy diet can make you feel sluggish and tired, which can worsen depression. In addition to improving physical health, exercise releases endorphins, chemicals that interact with receptors in the brain to create positive feelings.
- Avoid alcohol and drugs. Many substances may make you feel better for a short time but will ultimately make you feel worse and can lead to serious problems. They also may increase suicidal feelings or behavior.
- Ask for help. Some problems are too big for you to handle alone. Talk to a trusted adult family member, counselor, or doctor. If the person you confide in doesn't understand you at first, keep talking—to the same person or to someone else you trust. Don't be afraid to share your feelings honestly and to answer questions.

of it as an earnest suicide attempt because when the upper knot came untied and I fell, I just lay on the floor instead of redoing the knot." A doctor diagnosed Davis with major depression and anxiety. Between seeing a therapist and taking medication, Davis was able to overcome the cutting habit and his suicidal thoughts. He encourages teens who are cutting to seek help. "Even if you can't tell your family or friends, seek out a school or college therapist. Helping people deal with this stuff is their job."

DATING VIOLENCE

"When I was growing up, I watched my mother fall in and out of love with men who were nothing but bad for her," says Alexis O., a member of the National Youth Advisory Board for loveisrespect, an organization that promotes healthy, non-abusive teen relationships. "There was never a day when my mother and her man of the week weren't at each other's throats," she goes on. "I watched, day after day, as he verbally and physically abused her. Later in the day, she would go crawling back, because she thought no one else would want her—a thought put in her head by the same person who earlier called her a 'stupid slut.' I always knew somewhere deep down that their behavior was abnormal, and I swore to myself to never end up like my mother had."

Alexis managed to avoid the abusive relationships her mother endured. However, one out of every eleven teens reports being hit or physically hurt by a boyfriend or girlfriend. Dating violence—also called dating abuse or partner abuse—is any form of destructive behavior used to exert control over a dating partner. Teens who experience dating violence are more likely than their peers to become depressed and anxious, to start using drugs and alcohol, and to think about or attempt suicide. Many of these teens are afraid to tell anyone about their situation and are unsure where to turn for help. Compared to people who haven't experienced dating violence, victims of dating violence are twice as likely to attempt suicide multiple times.

Dating violence often begins early in life. About 22 percent of adult women report that they first experienced partner violence between the ages of eleven and seventeen. Such abuse takes several forms:

- Emotional: making threatening statements; shaming, bullying, insulting the partner; monitoring the partner's activities, or wanting to know where the partner is at all times; or controlling who the partner spends time with, including friends and family
- Physical: pinching, punching, hitting, shoving, slapping, or kicking

- Sexual: touching the partner in a way that makes the partner uncomfortable or forcing the partner into any unwanted sexual activity or threatening to do so
- Stalking: repeatedly harassing or threatening a partner to cause fear, through phone calls, e-mails, text messages and other forms of communication, or in person

Abusive behavior, especially in teen relationships, is not always obvious. Some children grow up believing violence is an acceptable part of relationships. Witnessing domestic violence in the home as a child, as Alexis did, is a major risk factor for experiencing dating violence later in life. This is true for both girls and boys. Physical violence is only one form of dating violence, however, and other forms can be harder to recognize. A partner may appear affectionate and considerate at certain times while displaying an explosive temper or extreme jealousy at other times. Some partners even claim that their controlling behavior is evidence of their deep love—and some genuinely believe this to be the truth.

A teen may not be certain whether a relationship is abusive, especially if other people she knows are in abusive relationships and consider them normal. An abusive partner usually displays manipulative or possessive behavior—such as checking the other partner's phone or e-mails without permission; limiting or expressing disapproval of the partner's interactions with other people; or pressuring the partner into doing something the other partner does not want to do, including having sex. Even if partners have had consensual sex before, a person has the right to say no to any sexual activity at any time and for any reason. If the person's partner does not respect that right, this constitutes abusive behavior.

Leaving a damaging relationship can be almost as devastating as being in one. Teens may find it difficult to break away from an abusive partner for a variety of reasons. A teen who has been emotionally abused by her partner may believe she is worthless or cannot survive without the relationship. A teen whose partner has physically abused or threatened her may fear the partner will retaliate after a breakup. Parents, friends, faith leaders, school counselors, and other trusted adults can help. In some cases, police involvement may be necessary. Ultimately, ending an abusive relationship reduces the risk of further harm, including the possibility of suicide.

"BULLYING CAN KILL"

On Michael Berry's seventeenth birthday in 2010, his third-period teacher at Mira Loma High School in Sacramento, California, gave him permission to leave his classroom to go to the bathroom. He never returned to class. Instead, after enduring months of vicious and relentless bullying, he shot himself in the head with a gun that he'd taken from his uncle's house.

The previous summer, a classmate had decided Michael was gay—and that this was cause for ridicule. The boy spread the rumor both online and by word of mouth. By the time the new school year started, kids were talking about Michael. The harassment continued constantly, at school and online. Rather than stepping up to help him, Michael's friends caved in to peer pressure and turned against him.

Michael didn't tell his parents what was happening, but he did

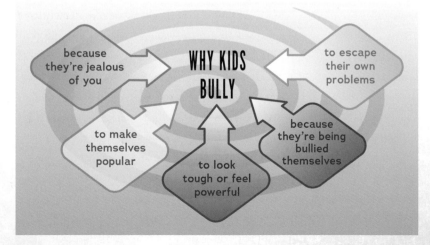

ask for help from school counselors and other staff members. When a reporter later asked if school staff had helped Michael, school spokesman Trent Allen said, "Any time we have a [bullying] question raised, we have an interest in investigating it fully. In this incident, [protocol] was followed. I can't share any outcomes of that, because it goes directly to student privacy."

Michael's mother, Lisa Ford-Berry, insisted that school staff had not done enough to protect her son. "He reported it," she recalled of the bullying episodes. "He went to his counselors on three separate occasions. He had a confirmed appointment with the vice-principal; Michael showed up for the appointment, and he was stood up. He circled back around to his teachers, and his fourth-period teacher, and . . . her advice was to ignore it." She said on a separate occasion, "Our boy fell through the cracks and broke under the pain."

In 2006 Megan Meier hanged herself in her closet just before her fourteenth birthday after a boy she'd befriended online insulted her, spread lies about her, and said that the world would be a better place without her. In fact, the verbally abusive boy was not a real person but a persona created by two adults—the parents of a friend who had argued with Megan. Megan was one of many teens to commit suicide after experiencing the cruelty of bullying. During 2014 and 2015 alone, numerous cases of bullied teens committing suicide surfaced in the media. Fifteen-year-old Simon Brooks of the United Kingdom poisoned himself. Twelve-year-old Rebecca Sedwick jumped off the roof of a cement factory in Florida. Fourteen-year-old Raymond Howell Jr. shot himself in Dallas, Texas, after being bullied online and in person. Twelve-year-old Ronin Shimizu, the only male cheerleader at his California middle school, took his life after months of antigay bullying. Fourteen-year-old Carla Jamerson of Las Vegas, Nevada, took her life in 2015 after years of bullying and counseling for depression. Like Michael Berry, they were driven to kill themselves by the abusive words and actions of their peers.

These teens were not alone in being bullied. Up to one-third of US students in grades six through twelve have been bullied at school, while 15 percent of high school students have experienced cyberbullying—

bullying via texts, e-mails, and social media. Bullying can be physical or verbal and can involve hitting, kicking, threats of violence, pranks, name-calling, and insults. While the vast majority of young people who are bullied do not take their own lives, bullying can lead to feelings of isolation, rejection, despair, anxiety, and depression, which in turn can contribute to suicidal behavior. A 2014 report by the CDC asserts that "bullying behavior and suicide-related behavior are closely related."

Youth activist e.E. Charlton-Trujillo echoes this perspective. "Kids who are bullied are up to nine times more likely to commit suicide," she says. "Translation? Bullying can kill. Hateful words that harass and demoralize—whether in person or posted online—can drive young people to suicide."

THE FIGHT AGAINST BULLYING

One 2007 study surveyed more than fifteen thousand American children and teens in elementary, middle, and high schools and found that about three out of ten students admitted to bullying others. Bullies may pick on people who seem different from them or who don't fit in. They may target others based on their race, religion, or sexual and gender orientation. Some bullies are themselves victims of bullying or are experiencing family violence. Bullies may be jealous, want to look tough, or believe that being a bully will make them more popular.

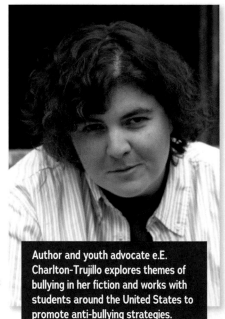

Author and youth advocate e.E. Charlton-Trujillo explores themes of bullying in her fiction and works with students around the United States to promote anti-bullying strategies.

Charlton-Trujillo advises young people to think carefully about the victims of bullying, especially those who have been driven to suicide. She says, "Really visualize them. Their smile. The way they laugh. The

TIPS FOR DEALING WITH BULLYING

Experts point to the following strategies for dealing with bullying.

If you are the victim of bullying:

- Know that it is not your fault. Don't feel that you have to change anything about yourself. Bullies' behavior is the result of their own situations and choices, not the result of anything you have done wrong or anything that is wrong with who you are.
- Learn to walk away. Bullies want to have power over you. Ignoring them often deprives them of that power.
- Tell a trusted adult. Don't be ashamed to seek help and support.

If you see someone else being bullied:

- Speak up. This can be as simple as asking what is going on. When friends and bystanders intervene, bullying often stops within seconds. If the situation doesn't improve or involves immediate danger, remove the bullied person (and yourself) from the area. Invite him to join your lunch table or to take a walk with you.
- Tell an adult authority figure. The bullying may not seem serious enough to call for adult involvement, but taking this step can prevent the situation from escalating. You are trying to keep someone safe.
- Offer support to the bullied person whenever you see an opportunity. Even if the person is not being bullied at the moment, ask how she is doing. Spend some extra time with her. Include her in an activity or do her a small favor. Gestures like these help counteract the effects of bullying.

first time you saw them cry. See them to their fullest, their coolest. Now here's the hard part. You can't text or call or send a Facebook message. There's no app to reach them because they took their own life. When you read about someone being bullied and committing suicide, the real of that is, it's someone's most absolute cared-for person. Suicide is a permanent end to what could have most likely been avoided."

To counteract the negative effects of bullying, some elementary schools provide anti-bullying programs. Students learn anti-bullying strategies through classroom lessons, meetings, and role-playing. Laurette Gaberman, a National Board certified teacher, describes the Steps to Respect program at the California school where she teaches fourth grade. "We participated in an anti-bullying pilot program in Sacramento County, California, in 2011 and tracked the progress of each school," she says. "We found that after six months, there was a significant change in the pilot groups' behavior that resulted in fewer suspensions and far fewer behavioral issues."

Gaberman adds, "The Steps to Respect program begins by focusing on friendship skills. We teach conflict resolution and empathy skills. Compromise and understanding become part of school culture. Next we teach students how to recognize and refuse bullying behaviors. There's an emphasis on defusing a bullying situation and reporting every incident. We encourage the students to stand up for what is just, and not to simply stand by while someone bullies another student. Once the students recognize they can do this, the whole school dynamic begins to change. It's very powerful."

The program has been so successful that Gaberman's school district adopted it for the entire school in 2012. In 2015 the school district adopted a similar program called It's Cool to be Kind. Teachers and other anti-bullying advocates hope that if children learn these skills at

BY THE NUMBERS

- An estimated 8 percent of high school students have attempted suicide.
- While girls attempt suicide twice as often as boys, boys are four times more likely to die.
- Suicide is the second-leading cause of death among young people.
- One out of three students say they have been bullied at school.

an early age, they will be much less likely to engage in bullying behavior in middle school and high school, creating a safer environment for young people and reducing the number of suicides related to bullying.

IT GETS BETTER

Many teens find it difficult to see beyond their immediate feelings of isolation or hopelessness. Although it may be impossible to believe, these problems generally improve in the long run. In the next few months, the next year, or by the end of high school, many of the struggles that young people face lessen and even disappear, while others, such as mental health issues, can be controlled.

Susan Caldwell, who lost her seventeen-year-old daughter Amy to suicide, urges teens to stop and think. "Don't take your own life. You can't imagine ever feeling good again when you're so depressed, but someday you will. Adolescence is one of the most difficult periods of life. When combined with depression, it's even harder. But you can recover from depression with the right medication and therapy. Don't give up the chance to live a fulfilling and happy life."

There are no do-overs when it comes to suicide. Those who have lost loved ones, those who have contemplated suicide and found another way out of their despair, and experts in suicide-related fields all urge teens not to make the tragic and irreversible decision to end their lives. As poet Meggie Royer wrote,

The morning after I killed myself, I went back to that body in the morgue and tried to talk some sense into her. I told her about the avocados and the stepping stones, the river and her parents. I told her about the sunsets and the dog and the beach.

The morning after I killed myself, I tried to unkill myself, but couldn't finish what I started.

Each of the 1,892 American flags placed on the National Mall represents one of the 1,892 veterans and service members who committed suicide in 2014.

Chapter 4

SUICIDE IN THE MILITARY

In July 2014, three families testified before the US House of Representatives Committee on Veterans' Affairs in a hearing called *Service Should Not Lead to Suicide*. The hearings had been organized in response to public outcry at the alarming numbers of US suicides among active duty service members and veterans who had served in the Iraq and Afghanistan conflicts. Susan and Richard Selke spoke of their son, Clay Hunt, a US Marines veteran who had served in Iraq and Afghanistan. After receiving an honorable discharge in 2009, he spiraled downward until he took his life in 2011 when he was twenty-eight. Peggy Portwine told of her son, Brian, also an Iraq veteran, who had served with the US Army and took his life in 2011 at the age of twenty-three. And Howard and Jean Somers talked about their son Daniel, who served in an intelligence unit in Iraq. He wrote a detailed suicide note before he shot himself in 2013 at the age of thirty.

According to the testimony of the parents, these three young men had each suffered a traumatic brain injury (TBI) and post-traumatic stress disorder (PTSD). TBI is any injury to the brain caused by an outside force, such as a blow to the head or the jolt caused by blast waves from bombs. PTSD is a mental health condition resulting from a traumatic or frightening event, such as being in battle, and can involve extreme anxiety, nightmares, and terrifying flashbacks.

Peggy Portwine testified that Brian had suffered multiple concussions and traumatic brain injury following several roadside bombings. "After coming home from his first deployment, Brian had trouble with short-term memory. When his friends were going somewhere, he would often say, 'Where are we going again? You know I have scrambled brains.' . . . In 2010 Brian was recalled to the army and sent back to Iraq for nearly a year. During his discharge, a counselor diagnosed Brian with PTSD, TBI, depression, and anxiety." Veterans qualify to receive treatment at veterans' hospitals after the military discharges them, but even though the military found Brian to be at high risk for suicide, his mother said he was not properly treated at the VA center he visited. She and the other parents testifying before the committee felt the US Department of Veterans Affairs (VA) had failed their sons. "The VA and DOD [Department of Defense] are doing a disservice to our young men and women," she said. "They're quick to send them [to war], but slow to treat them, if they treat them at all."

HOW COMMON IS VETERAN SUICIDE?

Prior to US military involvement in Iraq and Afghanistan, suicide among active duty service members was 25 percent lower than in the civilian (nonmilitary) population. However, between 2005 and 2009, suicides of US Army and US Marine personnel nearly doubled, according to a study published in the *Journal of the American Medical Association* in 2012. At least one out of five Americans who die by suicide is a veteran. The VA has reported that between eighteen and twenty-two veterans take their lives each day. However, many observers believe the actual number is far higher. The VA's report relied only on information from the first twenty-one states to contribute data to the project. Illinois, Texas, and California—states

The Veterans Administration has reported that between 18 and 22 veterans take their lives each day. Other authorities believe the number could be much higher.

with large veteran populations—were not among the states studied.

Additionally, many death certificates omit information about veteran status, making it difficult to track all veteran deaths. Perhaps most significant, many veteran suicides cannot be confirmed as such. In 2014 writers for the blog *Military Suicide Report* contended that in its report, the VA had "low-balled this often-quoted suicide [statistic] at a time when it had clear evidence showing that the number likely is closer to fifty a day, when one includes death by toxic drug overdose (pharmaceuticals and alcohol) and high-speed personal vehicle crashes (motorcycles included) that are more likely than not suicides." The article claimed that between 2001 and 2014, "[more than] one hundred thousand American veterans have died from suicide, according to data from both the VA and the CDC."

Iraq and Afghanistan Veterans of America (IAVA), a nonprofit veteran advocacy organization founded in 2004, said in 2014 that suicide and mental health issues were the top concerns its members face. Nearly one-third of IAVA's veteran members had thought about suicide since joining the military, and four out of ten knew a veteran who had died by suicide.

While the exact statistics for military suicide rates remain up for debate, government and military authorities acknowledge that suicide is a significant problem among veterans. Caleb S. Cage, who served as a US Army captain in Iraq and is a former executive director of the Nevada Department of Veterans Services, is very familiar with veteran suicide. "Military and veteran suicide is such an issue because it has a huge impact on the individual, family, and community," he says.

RISK FACTORS FOR VETERAN SUICIDES

Why do so many military veterans and active duty service members commit suicide? Common sense might suggest that the stress of war overwhelms some people, fueling feelings of exhaustion, guilt, or insecurity and triggering mental health issues such as depression, all of which may lead to suicide. Yet the reality is less clear. One DOD report showed that 85 percent of veterans who took their lives in 2011 had not seen combat, and about half had never been deployed. A 2013 study by the *Journal of the American Medical Association* reviewed data from 151,560 military personnel in all branches of the US military, including the Reserve and National Guard, and found that deployment or combat could not be linked to increased suicide rates. Instead, factors associated with a significantly higher risk of suicide included being male, being depressed, having bipolar disorder, and experiencing alcohol-related problems. Another article—published in 2014 and based on several studies—suggested that affiliation with the military may not increase the risk of suicide but that more suicidal people join.

A report published by the US Department of Defense (DOD) in 2014 described the profile of the typical active duty service member who attempted or completed suicide in 2013. That person was male, white/Caucasian, non-Hispanic, under thirty years old, junior enlisted (not an officer), and a high school graduate. Both male and female service members are at risk for suicide. While more male service members than female service members commit suicide, this is because far more men than women serve in the military. Female veterans take their own lives nearly six times more often than do women who have not served in the military, according to research released in June 2015. "It's staggering," says Matthew Miller, an epidemiologist (a doctor who studies the patterns, causes, and effects of diseases and other health conditions) and suicide expert at Northeastern University in Boston. "We have to come to grips with why the rates are so obscenely high."

VA experts are not certain what's behind the high rates of female military suicide. Aside from the traumas and strains that veterans of both sexes face, women are more likely than men to endure sexual harassment and rape during military service. The US government estimates that 10 percent of women have been raped during their service. The actual number could be much higher. It's also possible that the military draws women who are at higher risk for suicide.

"It was at the point where you have a gun up to your head, you can taste the carbon of a barrel in your mouth, and the only thing that stands between me and being a statistic is 4.5 pounds [2 kilograms] of trigger pressure."

—Justin Fitch, US Army captain, 2014

Numerous studies have linked TBI and PTSD to a high risk of suicide. Tens of thousands of military members have experienced TBI, which can range in severity from a simple concussion (a mild brain injury that can result in temporary pain or disorientation) to a coma (a state of prolonged unconsciousness due to severe brain injury). The DOD estimates that from January 2000 through March 31, 2015, doctors diagnosed 333,169 TBIs in members of the military. The major causes of TBI in the military are penetrating injuries(when a bullet or flying debris such as shrapnel pierces the skull and enters the brain) and blast injuries (when an explosion sends a high-speed blast wave through the brain faster than the speed of sound, severely damaging brain cells and nerve pathways).

PTSD is a mental health condition that can occur after traumatic events, such as accidents, assaults, natural disasters, and war. The symptoms of PTSD include depression, feelings of hopelessness, insomnia, and flashbacks—vivid, uncontrollable, and terrifying memories of traumatic events. PTSD can affect people's ability to concentrate, their impulse control, and their relationships with others. The US Department of Veterans Affairs estimates that between 11 and 20 percent of those who fought in Iraq or Afghanistan—about twice as high a percentage as in the civilian population—suffer PTSD. Many service members who experienced TBI suffer PTSD as well, a

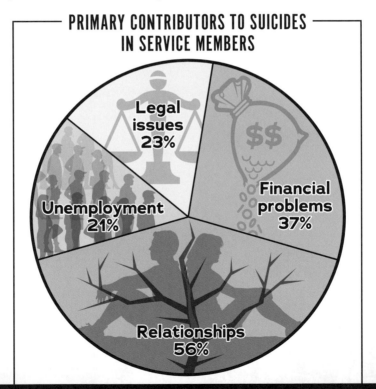

PRIMARY CONTRIBUTORS TO SUICIDES IN SERVICE MEMBERS

Legal issues 23%

Financial problems 37%

Unemployment 21%

Relationships 56%

The United States Army Reserve Command (USARC) Case Review Work Group calculated the main stressors involved in Army Reserve suicides in 2013. Many suicides involved more than one of these stressors. For example, of the 56 percent of studied reservists who faced relationship stressors, many also dealt with one or more other primary stressors, as shown in the percentages above.

WARNING SIGNS FOR VETERAN SUICIDE

The national nonprofit organization Stop Soldier Suicide lists these warning signs that a veteran may be at risk for suicide:

- Feelings of isolation from family and friends or of being a burden to others
- Financial, medical, legal, work-related, or relationship problems
- Substance abuse
- Problems with a major life transition, such as divorce, discharge from the military, or retirement
- The death of a fellow soldier or a veteran friend
- Feelings of being a burden to others

combination that could put them at even higher risk for self-harm.

Still, the large numbers of service members with TBI and PTSD do not fully explain the prevalence of military suicides. Studies suggest a wide range of issues are at play. A 2014 report by the DOD found that the youngest soldiers in the US Army Reserve—those between seventeen and twenty-four years old—had a higher rate of suicide than older active duty service members. The report found that relationship troubles, unemployment, financial concerns, and legal problems were the primary stressors causing suicide in these younger service members.

Richard Doss, a psychologist working in military suicide prevention, believes that younger people have not yet developed coping strategies for the challenges of military and civilian life. "They [young soldiers] recently left home and are establishing themselves as adults," notes Doss. "They come from a military environment where many decisions are made for them and [when they return home] they have to make their own decisions. It can be overwhelming."

BARRIERS AND MYTHS

Many service members are reluctant to seek care for emotional problems, especially mental health issues. Some fear the stigma of mental illness may damage their career or cause others to lose confidence in their abilities. About 86 percent of active duty service members are male, and men in general are often hesitant to seek help for emotional and psychological issues because they may view it as a sign of weakness and an inability to cope with life.

A 2014 report by the American Psychological Association concluded that military suicides are strongly linked to experiences and issues that preceded military service: "Soldiers who reported abuse as children were three to eight times more likely than those who were not abused to report suicidal behavior; and both [active duty] service members and veterans who attempted suicide before joining the military were six times more likely to attempt suicide after entering the service than those who had never attempted suicide."

Yet many people misunderstand the profile of military suicides. *The Washington Post* published an article in 2014 describing the following five common myths about military suicide:

- *Myth: Suicides have increased because the military has overstretched its troops by sending them on multiple tours of duty.* Redeployment of troops who have already served in a combat zone is commonly believed to take an emotional and physical toll that drives more veterans to suicide. However, several large studies have shown suicide rates are higher for those who have never been deployed and for those without combat experience than for those who have seen combat. About one-third of soldiers who attempted suicide between 2004 and 2009 had mental health disorders before enlisting.

- *Myth: Suicides will decline with the end of US military involvement in Iraq and Afghanistan.* The last US combat forces left Iraq in 2011, and the pullout in Afghanistan is well under way and due to be complete by the end of 2017, yet studies show no decline in military suicide rates. In fact, a 2015 DOD report found that the number of suicides among active duty service members remained at historically high levels for the fifth year in a row.

- *Myth: Suicides have increased because the military lowered recruitment standards and forced soldiers to stay on active duty for longer periods of time.* During the height of the Iraq war, the military made some exceptions to its usual enlistment qualifications, accepting recruits with medical concerns, criminal histories, and histories of substance use that would have barred them from service at other times. The military also extended many troops' tours of duty. However, the army has not found that these factors pushed up the suicide rate.

- *Myth: The weakest troops—those with poor coping skills—are most at risk.* Data does not support this belief. Members of elite units such as Army Rangers and Navy SEALs, traditionally selected for their mental and physical toughness—according to Admiral William McRaven, who was in charge of the United States Special Operations Command from 2011 to 2014—are also taking their lives in record numbers.

- *Myth: This is a problem unique to the military.* The military reflects the society in which its service members live. Factors such as substance abuse and mental illness are linked to civilian suicides as well as military suicides.

While suicides among active duty members and veterans are high, studies show that the risk of suicide is also high among the families of veterans and active duty members. A study published in 2015, using data from California teens who took part in the California Healthy Kids Survey, showed that teens connected with military families were at greater risk of suicide than teens with no military connection. Nearly 12 percent of those teens reported attempting suicide, compared to

7.3 percent of teens with no military connections. The study suggests that to help prevent suicide among teens with military connections, institutions need to be on the lookout for such teens in the populations they serve. The study says, "Primary health care providers, mental health providers, schools, and other community organizations should work to increase their awareness of the presence of military-connected youth and families that they serve."

A PUSH FOR CHANGE

In 2014 VA hospitals across the United States came under intense scrutiny after insiders leaked information to the media about negligence in patient care. Veterans who had been on long waiting lists to receive treatment—often waiting several months for an appointment—had died before receiving the care they needed. At least two of these deaths were confirmed suicides, according to Margaret Moxness, a doctor who worked at a VA medical center in Charleston, West Virginia. The VA is making changes to its system to decrease veteran suicides.

"The Department of Veterans Affairs has invested heavily to decrease military suicides," says veteran advocate Caleb Cage. "It has increased mental health counselors and has established a national military and veteran crisis phone and text line. The Department is working to decrease barriers for the diagnosis and treatment of PTSD, and to reduce the stigma of accessing mental health care." Cage adds that other agencies, such as the US government's Substance Abuse and Mental Health Services Administration, are working on this cause as well.

As part of the effort to improve care, each branch of the military has instituted at least one suicide prevention program. Numerous government and civilian websites devoted to mental health and suicide prevention target the military and veteran community. Twenty-four-hour crisis helplines are available by phone and text. Confidential online chats offer immediate connection with people who can help. Families can access resources to help cope with troubled veterans. But is this enough?

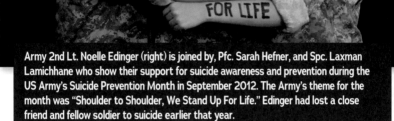

Army 2nd Lt. Noelle Edinger (right) is joined by, Pfc. Sarah Hefner, and Spc. Laxman Lamichhane who show their support for suicide awareness and prevention during the US Army's Suicide Prevention Month in September 2012. The Army's theme for the month was "Shoulder to Shoulder, We Stand Up For Life." Edinger had lost a close friend and fellow soldier to suicide earlier that year.

Advocates say that more must be done to ensure that service members have timely access to health care, rather than having to wait months for appointments and treatment. Some observers recommend that primary health-care providers—those in private practice as well as at VA facilities—consistently screen veterans and active duty service members for mental health issues in every setting, such as during routine medical appointments in doctors' offices and clinics. Just as important is maintaining and strengthening the protective effects of connections with family, friends, and fellow veterans.

SUICIDE PREVENTION LEGISLATION

In February 2015, a study of more than one million veterans showed that the suicide rate among veterans remains about 50 percent higher than that of the general population. That same month, President Barack Obama signed the Clay Hunt Suicide Prevention for American Veterans Act. Months earlier, Clay Hunt's parents had testified before the House Committee on Veterans' Affairs about their son's suicide.

"Today we honor a young man who isn't here but should be here," President Obama said at the signing ceremony. "Everyone can do more, with and for our veterans. This [preventing veteran suicide] has to be a national mission."

According to the IAVA, the act aims to reduce veteran and military suicide by improving access to high-quality mental health care. The act's provisions include the creation of peer support and community outreach programs to assist service members' transition to civilian life. The law offers financial aid to medical students specializing in psychiatry to help recruit more psychiatrists to practice in the VA system. To ensure accountability, the law requires an annual evaluation of VA mental health and suicide prevention programs. Improving VA mental health services is a crucial step. A ten-year study of nearly 174,000 military suicides showed that the suicide rate of veterans who used VA services was significantly lower than veterans who did not use VA services.

Caleb Cage supports such programs but also stresses that treatment and support must exist beyond the national level. "I personally believe that the most important work is being done at the state and community levels where peer-to-peer activities are under way. Offices of Suicide

VETERAN SUICIDE PREVENTION FILM WINS AN OSCAR

The 2015 Academy Award for best short documentary went to *Crisis Hotline: Veterans Press 1*, a forty-minute film about a veterans' suicide hotline. Filmed at a Veterans Affairs center in New York, the documentary follows well-trained volunteers and former veterans who take one thousand calls each day from veterans, active duty service members, and their families. Some callers are on the brink of suicide. Other callers are family members who are terrified their loved ones might take their own lives. The crisis hotline has handled more than 1.3 million calls and has saved an estimated forty-two thousand lives since it was launched in 2007.

Prevention are implementing state plans that include elements for military members and veterans. States are also able to track data better to measure effectiveness of their efforts. The federal resources are valuable and are well coordinated at the national level. However, the work that will change people's lives is most often accomplished in the communities where they live."

Suicide prevention is a top priority for the military, according to DOD spokeswoman Cynthia Smith. "Our most valuable resource within the department is our people," she said. "We are committed to taking care of our people, and that includes doing everything possible to prevent suicides in the military."

While many suicidal veterans can benefit from professional help, ultimately they also rely on support and understanding from family members, friends, and even strangers. Ask former Massachusetts National Guard sergeant Nate Radke. After returning from a deployment to Afghanistan, Radke's business was not doing well. His family life was unhappy. Suffering from both PTSD and TBI, he had difficulty getting the treatment he needed and waited a long time for medical appointments at his local VA. The government also denied his application for Social Security disability benefits. One night in 2012, Radke consumed a large amount of pills and alcohol and sped off in his car, intending to drive into a tree and kill himself. Moments before he carried out his plan, a police officer pulled Radke over for speeding. When the officer approached, Radke started talking. "'Well, it's not worth living anymore, you know?' I told him. I opened up to him. Because I was literally two minutes away from killing myself." The officer took Radke to a nearby hospital and checked him in.

That was the beginning of a new life for Radke. Admitting that he'd planned to take his life gave him a chance to connect with people who wanted to help. For example, Radke worked with Sergeant-Major Bill Davidson, who runs a program for the Army National Guard designed to decrease suicide among soldiers. Advocates also connected Radke to services that helped him find housing and counseling for him and his wife.

Radke later worked with the National Guard to make a training video in which he tells his story. "If you're thinking about suicide, ask for help. [Asking for help is] not making you weak. It's making you strong." Radke is deeply grateful that someone reached out to him when he needed help, and he hopes to offer the same lifeline to others. "Now I'm in a situation to give. I've been helping other veterans."

BY THE NUMBERS

- The military estimates between eighteen and twenty-two veterans take their lives by suicide each day. Other sources say the numbers could be much higher.
- PTSD, a known risk factor for suicide, is twice as high among members of the military as in the civilian population.
- The suicide rate among veterans and military members is about 50 percent higher than in the civilian population.

Chapter 5

ADULT SUICIDE

Domenica Di Piazza, an editor who works in nonfiction publishing for teens, returned from a late-night dinner in 2002 to find an unexpected message on her phone. It was from the coroner's office in the town where her mother, Lytton Davis, lived. "I imagined my mother had died in a car accident," Domenica said. Before she could return the call, Domenica's brother phoned to say that he had already spoken with the coroner. "My brother had few details other than that my mother had been found dead in her apartment that afternoon. Worried neighbors, who had not seen her in several days, had called the police. The authorities discovered her on the bed with a gun on her chest."

Domenica explains, "It's hard to know precisely what triggered my mother's decision to take her life that particular day. She had a long history of undiagnosed psychiatric difficulties. In the 1950s, a doctor had put her on Valium, a common prescription at the time for 'unstable' women." Yet Lytton was intelligent, charming, and high-functioning. After divorcing Domenica's father in the mid-1970s, Lytton worked at a major university for several years where she held administrative positions in the women's studies and the African American studies departments. "Over the years, my mother struggled with mood swings, depression, and crippling anxiety. About ten years before her suicide, a doctor diagnosed her with cyclothymia, a mild form of bipolar disorder."

Domenica believes her mother's final decline started with the death of her own mother, which triggered a withdrawal from her social networks and support systems. "She pulled away from the workplace, which in many ways had been a lifeline, a connection to friendships and the outer world." Domenica's mother also faced financial problems and health issues. Domenica remembers the aftermath of her mother's death. "In the first couple of years after my mother's suicide, all I could think about and dream about and talk about was my mother's death. My sister and I would meet every Tuesday for dinner at our favorite bistro, and we talked of only one thing: our mother's life and her suicide. In looking back, it's so strange that I never thought my mother would actually take her own life. She had expressed suicidal thoughts out loud over the years, but I had always put it down to fantastical thinking. I didn't think a person's mother could take her own life."

PROFILE OF A SUICIDE

Domenica's mother, Lytton, was sixty-eight years old when she took her life. While suicide among young people often attracts media attention, the highest rate of suicide actually occurs in middle-aged and elderly people. Lenny Bernstein and Lena H. Sun, journalists for the *Washington Post*, wrote that a profile of a person at high risk for suicide would look like this: "a middle-aged or older white male toward the end of a successful career, who suffers from a serious medical problem as well as chronic depression and substance abuse, who recently completed treatment for either or both of those psychological conditions, and who is going through a difficult period, personally or professionally."

Writing shortly after comedian and actor Robin Williams took his life in 2014 at the age of sixty-three, Bernstein and Sun noted that Williams was a near-perfect match for their profile. Producers had canceled Williams's new TV series, *The Crazy Ones*, after it attracted few viewers. He was rumored to have financial problems. He struggled with severe depression and had recently finished an addiction treatment program. He had a history of heart surgery, and he had recently been diagnosed with Parkinson's disease (though this may have been a misdiagnosis of the neurological disease Lewy Body dementia, which has some similar symptoms). In cases such as Williams's, a combination of problems can strain a person's coping ability beyond its limits.

> The highest rate of suicide is among middle-aged people aged forty-five to sixty-four years old. Elderly people—those who are eighty-five and older—have the second-highest rate of suicide.

RISK FACTORS FOR OLDER ADULTS

While adults over the age of sixty-five make up 12 percent of the population, they account for 18 percent of suicide deaths in the United States. The highest rate of suicide is among middle-aged people aged forty-five to sixty-four years old. Elderly people—those who are eighty-five and older—have the second-highest rate of suicide. An estimated 20 percent of adults over the age of fifty-five live with a mental health issue, yet most never seek treatment, even when it's available.

A 2015 report published in the *American Journal of Preventive Medicine* found that the suicide rate for Americans between forty and sixty-four years of age has risen about 40 percent since 1999. Researchers found that money problems affected more than one-third of those who died by suicide in the year 2010. "Relative to other age groups, a larger and increasing proportion of middle-aged suicides have circumstances associated with job, financial, or legal distress," said study authors Katherine A. Hempstead and Julie A. Phillips.

DEATH BY BRIDGE

Bridges around the world are suicide magnets. Jumping from a high bridge is very likely, although not certain, to result in death. Some bridges, such as San Francisco's Golden Gate Bridge, have garnered significant media attention, making it more likely that people will choose these as places to take their lives. At least seventeen hundred people have died after jumping off the Golden Gate Bridge. That number is almost certainly higher because the bodies of some jumpers are never found. Additionally, police officers and passersby stop hundreds of others on the verge of jumping. Signs offering crisis counseling are posted along the bridge. Free call boxes connect suicidal persons to crisis counselors. In 2014 city officials approved a steel suicide-prevention net to hang beneath the bridge to catch anyone who jumps. The net should be in place by 2018. Kevin Hines, who survived his jump from the Golden Gate Bridge when he was nineteen, said in an interview for NPR that such a net "would have stopped me from jumping."

Authorities are considering installing similar nets on the George Washington Bridge, which connects Manhattan, New York, to Fort Lee, New Jersey, and on the Rio Grande Gorge Bridge in Taos, New Mexico. Experts say such barriers are very effective at stopping suicides, since many suicides are impulsive. Psychologist Jill Harkavy-Friedman says, "When someone is in a suicidal crisis, their thinking is very fixed and they have tunnel vision. What a barrier does is give time for the crisis to pass and for help to arrive."

Signs such as this one posted on the Golden Gate Bridge in California offer alternatives to people who are considering suicide attempts. Experts believe these resources reduce the number of people who attempt suicide by jumping off bridges.

CRISIS COUNSELING
THERE IS HOPE
MAKE THE CALL

THE CONSEQUENCES OF JUMPING FROM THIS BRIDGE ARE FATAL AND TRAGIC.

"Financial difficulties related to the loss of retirement savings in the stock market crash [the economic downturn from 2007 to 2011] may explain some of this trend."

Risk factors for suicide in older adults include serious medical conditions, divorce, social isolation, poor sleep quality, and depression. Yet depression in older people often goes untreated. Some older people may view the onset of depression as a normal sign of aging. Others who have already lived with depression for many years may believe that they have their condition under control or that treatment can't help them. Yet studies show that the majority of people in this age group who struggle with depression can improve with treatment.

Warning signs of possible suicidal intent among older people can include the following:

- Loss of interest in previously enjoyable activities
- Stopping medical treatment such as a special diet or medications
- Stockpiling medications (pain or sleeping pills, for example)
- Giving away cherished personal items
- Putting financial affairs in order, such as creating new wills

If you see these behaviors in a parent or grandparent, an aunt or uncle, or a friend or neighbor, speak up. Ask what's wrong. Ask if you can help. Tell another trusted adult.

DO WE HAVE THE RIGHT TO DIE?

Imagine years of severe pain from crippling arthritis in your hands and knees. Imagine losing one-third of your tongue to cancer and being left with even more pain from radiation and surgery. Imagine having back pain with every step you take because a bone is pressing on nerves. Imagine spending every day and night in pain and being in a deep, dark depression that never goes away. That's what life looked like for Kerri Wagner when she attempted suicide in 2012 at the age of sixty-three.

Kerri was convinced her health would not improve and the pain would continue indefinitely. "I had struggled for years with pain and depression and knew there would simply be no relief," she recalls. "And so, having thought the event out, I tried to end my life. My only reluctance in taking the pills was leaving my husband alone. One Saturday night, I ingested fifty OxyContin tablets and about forty-five Valiums. My husband discovered me the next morning barely breathing, and called for an ambulance. I remained in the intensive care unit for about a week, five days of it in an induced coma on life support."

Kerri promised her husband she wouldn't try to kill herself again without talking it over with him first. The next year, they moved to Santa Fe, New Mexico, a place they enjoy. Even though life is better for Kerri, she maintains that her suicide attempt was an appropriate response to her condition at the time. "I believe the right to choose the time and nature of your passing is a personal choice and should be universally available," she says. "There are some people who just don't want to soldier on, and I'm one of them. The day will come when I will take my own path once more."

> "I woke up in the hospital surrounded by doctors and nurses yelling at me, demanding to know what I'd taken, even though my brain was barely working. I was bitter and angry that my husband found me in time to stop my suicide."
>
> —Kerri Wagner, speaking of her suicide attempt in 2012

Kerri attempted to take her life on her own, using stockpiled prescription medications. Others seek help from family members or their physicians. Physician-assisted suicide occurs when a practicing doctor assists a patient's death by providing information or tools—such as a prescription for a lethal dose of medication—to a patient who intends to commit suicide. Physician-assisted suicide is legal in Oregon, Washington, Vermont, and California. It is also legal by individual court ruling in Montana and in one county in New Mexico.

Why do people like Kerri Wagner wish to kill themselves? Most suffer from serious medical conditions with little chance of improvement. Nine out of ten people who choose physician-assisted suicide are older than fifty-five, and nearly eight out of ten have cancer. Others have heart or lung disease, suffer unrelenting pain, or have lost control of their bodily functions. They are no longer able to do the things they once loved and that gave their lives meaning, and they consider their quality of life to be so poor they see no reason to continue living.

To receive legal end-of-life medication in Oregon, for example, the patient must be eighteen years or older, be capable of making health-care decisions, have a terminal disease that will lead to death within six months, have a written request signed by at least two witnesses, and wait fifteen days to fill the prescription. The patient can cancel the request at any time. More than 750 people in Oregon have taken a lethal dose of medication since the state's Death with Dignity Act passed in 1997.

Supporters of the Oregon law say that patients should have a right to choose how they die if they are terminally ill. That's why Brittany Maynard and her husband moved from California to Oregon in 2014. Twenty-nine-year-old Brittany was far younger than the typical patient seeking physician-assisted suicide. However, she had been diagnosed with advanced glioblastoma, an aggressive and fatal brain tumor. A doctor told her she had six months to live. "I've discussed with many experts how I would die from it and it's a terrible, terrible way to die," Brittany said in an October 2014 interview. "So being able to choose to go with dignity is less terrifying." After talking with her family, she said, "there isn't a single person that loves me that wishes me more pain and more suffering."

Brittany Maynard's decision to die by physician-assisted suicide at a time and place of her choosing brought the right-to-die issue into

Brittany Maynard and her husband Dan Diaz at their wedding. After Maynard was diagnosed with incurable brain cancer, she and Diaz moved from California to Oregon in 2014 so that she could legally undergo physician-assisted suicide.

the public spotlight. Before her death in November 2014, Brittany advocated publicly for this right. In January 2015, her parents met with the California legislature to promote right-to-die laws in Brittany's former home state. In March 2015, Brittany's husband released a video that Brittany recorded before her death and in which she spoke out in support of a new California law. Many of her fellow Californians shared her outlook. In fact, polls show that the majority of California residents have long supported physician-assisted death. In an unexpected move, the California Medical Association dropped its thirty years of opposition to physician-assisted suicide in May 2015. In September 2015, the California legislature approved a physician-assisted suicide bill titled the End of Life Option Act, which

Governor Jerry Brown signed into law on October 5, 2015.

The issue resonates beyond US borders. Physician-assisted suicide is legal in some form in several European countries—Belgium, Germany, Luxembourg, the Netherlands, and Switzerland—and is being considered in other countries. World-renowned physicist Stephen Hawking, who suffers from a rare form of amyotrophic lateral sclerosis (also called Lou Gehrig's disease), announced to the media in June 2015 that he supports assisted suicide, which is illegal in the United Kingdom, where he lives. Hawking, who is almost completely paralyzed by his disease, said, "To keep someone alive against their wishes is the ultimate indignity." While he was not currently contemplating such a move, he added. "I would consider assisted suicide only if I were in great pain or felt I had nothing more to contribute but was just a burden to those around me." Those who feel they have reached that point deserve to end their lives on their own terms, Hawking emphasized. "We should not take away the freedom of the individual to choose to die."

Supporters of right-to-die laws say that people deserve to make this

JACK KEVORKIAN: HERO OR CRIMINAL?

Jack Kevorkian was a physician in Michigan who helped more than 130 people with terminal illnesses take their own lives between 1990 and 1998. Called Dr. Death by some, he publicly supported a patient's right to die. Kevorkian invented a machine he used with some patients to inject lethal doses of intravenous medications into the bloodstream. For other patients, he used a machine he had invented to deliver lethal amounts of carbon monoxide, an odorless and tasteless poisonous gas.

While his patients and their families may have viewed him as a hero, many others considered him a criminal, and he was convicted of murder in 1999. Kevorkian spent eight years in prison and ultimately died in 2011 from complications of liver cancer. About his actions, Kevorkian often said, "Dying is not a crime."

decision for themselves and that legalizing the process ensures clarity in laws and prevention of questionable or inefficient methods. Having laws on the books can ensure safeguards, such as mandatory reporting and state oversight, which prevent the practice from being abused. Furthermore, advocates point out that people may change their minds at any time and instead opt to receive traditional end-of-life care that includes comfort measures and pain medications.

Patients and their families already have the right to withdraw life-support measures when there is little or no hope of recovery. Advocates say assisted suicide is simply the next logical step in giving patients control over these situations. A 2014 survey that included more than seventeen thousand US doctors showed that 54 percent supported physician-assisted suicide, up from 46 percent in 2010. Advocacy groups hope to see assisted suicide become more widely accepted in the medical field and legalized in more states.

Even so, laws allowing physician-assisted suicide are unlikely to become widespread in the near future. Many people oppose these laws on religious or ethical grounds, insisting that no life should be ended prematurely. Other opponents respect the right-to-die movement's goal of ending unwanted suffering but believe that people could abuse the practice. For instance, family members burdened with a sick relative's long-term care might pressure the patient to commit suicide. Another fear is that insurance companies, which pay large expenses for the care of terminally ill people, may encourage or even suggest physician-assisted suicide because this option is less costly than ongoing medical care. Low-income patients may be particularly at risk for these abuses. The advocacy group Californians Against Assisted Suicide said in a 2015 statement, "End-of-life treatment options are already limited for millions of people—constrained by poverty, disability discrimination, and other obstacles. Adding this so-called 'choice' into our dysfunctional healthcare system will push people into [using] cheaper lethal options."

Opponents of assisted suicide also say that it's difficult to predict whether certain health conditions and treatments for them may improve and that suicide may be premature or unnecessary in those cases. For these reasons, many medical organizations oppose right-to-die laws. The American Medical Association (AMA), for example, says, "Instead of participating in assisted suicide, physicians must aggressively respond to the needs of patients at the end of life. Patients should not be abandoned once it is determined that [a] cure is impossible." Rather than resorting to assisting suicide, the AMA recommends that physicians use specialized and hospice care, support from faith leaders, family counseling, and other means of easing patients' suffering and preparing them for a natural death.

BY THE NUMBERS

- The highest rate of suicide is among people aged forty-five to sixty-four years old.
- About 20 percent of older adults live with mental health issues, yet most never seek treatment.
- Eight out of ten people who elect physician-assisted suicide have cancer.

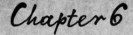

Chapter 6

A CHILD SAVED:
INTERVENTION AND TREATMENT SAVES LIVES

Kendra Pope asked her fifteen-year-old son, Paul, if he wanted to watch a movie with the family one April night in 2014. He refused and instead went to his bedroom. "Three hours later I went upstairs to give Paul his medications," Kendra says, "but he lay on his bed, having ingested two hundred of his antidepressant tablets and several tablets each of three other medications. He'd written a note that said, 'Life without happiness isn't living.' I called my husband and we flew down the stairs to the car and took Paul to the emergency room. We were there in five minutes."

At the hospital, Paul's heart stopped and medical staff had to defibrillate him (deliver an electric shock to his heart). "We watched him writhe like a snake, eyes wide open but not seeing, his pupils dilated to the size of dimes. He was in the middle of endless seizures which continued for several days."

Kendra and her husband had adopted Paul as a newborn. His biological parents both suffered from depression. Paul was a smart child and seemed stable and happy until third grade, when he bullied another child so badly that the child left school. Paul's parents immediately realized that their son needed help, and they began taking Paul to therapy. Kendra made sure Paul took the medications for depression that the therapist prescribed for him. Later, the family tried group therapy, although Paul refused to attend after he turned fourteen. As Paul grew older, the diagnoses piled up: attention deficit/hyperactivity disorder, mild depression, severe depression, anxiety, oppositional defiant disorder, and high-functioning autism.

Paul attacked his father one night in anger. In another incident, he broke his brother's nose. Twice, Paul's parents had to call the police because of Paul's violence, resulting in two psychiatric hospitalizations for Paul. At one point, he was admitted to a psychiatric wilderness program that mixed therapy with challenging outdoor experiences. However, the program kicked Paul out within two weeks after he hit a counselor in the head with a rock. His parents moved him to a neuropsychiatric institute where he stayed for more than a month.

The Popes refused to give up on Paul. They continued to offer him unconditional love and support while searching for the best place for him to get treatment. After surviving his suicide attempt in 2014, Paul moved to a residential treatment facility, a program that provides on-site housing and therapy for people with substance abuse, mental illness, and behavioral problems.

"This is a high-security place with a lot of counseling—individual, group, and family therapy, plus attending school," Kendra says. "Doctors are still tweaking Paul's medications. He's doing exceptionally well there and will be coming home soon. We'll continue with family and individual therapy." Kendra is hopeful about the future. "Paul came home for two short visits that went well. However, I have no illusion that he is cured. This is a lifelong problem and Paul will be in a constant state of recovery. I'm not sure how he'll cope with the stress of normal life, but I'm praying and hoping that my son chooses life."

Recognizing and treating emotional problems and mental illness as early as possible can decrease the risk of suicide and improve the chance for recovery. A wide variety of treatment options exist to help people meet their specific needs.

THERAPY AND COUNSELING

Several kinds of health-care professionals receive special training that allows them to provide therapy (sometimes called talk therapy or psychotherapy) to patients with mental health and substance abuse disorders. Types of therapists include the following:

- **Psychiatrists** are medical doctors who specialize in diagnosing and treating mental illness. Psychiatrists prescribe medication, and some provide counseling as well.
- **Psychiatric and mental health nurse practitioners** have advanced degrees and may provide counseling. In some states, they are permitted to prescribe medications.
- **Psychologists** have doctorates (PhDs) in psychology. Psychologists receive specialized training in diagnosing mental issues and treating them, but in most states, they are not legally allowed to prescribe medications.
- **Social workers** with master's degrees and specialized training may diagnose patients and provide therapy or counseling, but they may not legally prescribe medications.

Regular meetings with therapists provide focused help to patients. Therapy services are available at mental health provider offices, school and college counseling offices, and community and county mental health clinics. Patients may see therapists alone, with their families (family therapy), or with others who have a similar diagnosis (group therapy). Therapy helps people to understand how their moods, thoughts, and behaviors influence their lives. Therapists help clients build strategies for reorganizing their thinking and behaviors to better manage stress and other challenges.

One-on-one talk therapy is one treatment option for people coping with suicide risk factors such as depression, anxiety, and other mental health issues.

"Feeling suicidal can be a side effect of depression, anxiety, trauma, and other life challenges," says Dr. Ann Steiner, a psychologist, author, and professional speaker who leads therapy groups. "Groups offer a place for members to help each other figure out what's triggering their self-destructive thoughts. Members support each other and help one another make healthier decisions. Group therapy is the antidote for isolation. It's a safe place for members to speak honestly about their feelings and to discover that they have valuable perspectives and experiences to share. Members of long-term groups often say that group therapy feels like having a family you get to choose, a soft place to land."

Different types of therapy aim to help people struggling with specific issues. For instance, cognitive behavior therapy helps people understand how their own thoughts and feelings influence their behavior, while interpersonal therapy addresses their relationships with other people. Short-term therapy generally lasts three to four months. Some patients may require long-term therapy to achieve or maintain wellness over a matter of years or even a lifetime.

Mental health therapist Chris Crutcher recommends "a therapy group of like-minded kids run by a skilled therapist" for teens who might be thinking of suicide. "The connection piece and the 'you-are-not-alone' piece are hugely important. And I always recommend vigorous physical exercise. Most kids who want to die feel powerless to influence their own outcomes. Anything I can get them doing that empowers them is gold, and the physical is as important as the emotional. In fact, they're inseparable."

For people who are not in therapy or who cannot access their usual support systems when a crisis arises, emergency counseling can be a lifesaving resource. Telephone crisis lines, such as the National Suicide Prevention Lifeline, (800) 273-8255, are available at all times. Some organizations and health insurers also offer phone counseling. People in need also have the option of participating

Many people at risk for suicide find support and empowerment in group therapy sessions, where they interact with people who are facing similar stressors.

in interactive online counseling such as the one for service members and their families at Military OneSource (http://www.militaryonesource.mil). The American Foundation for Suicide Prevention (https://www.afsp.org) offers web-based assessments to universities and workplaces that allow trained counselors to review students' or employees' results and offer anonymous online or telephone interaction with people who wish to participate.

> "When two-thirds of the people who do have access to mental health [care] never take advantage of it because of the stigma associated with it, that's a real problem. . . . Everybody needs a checkup from the neck up."
>
> —Patrick J. Kennedy, former Rhode Island congressman who lives with bipolar disorder

MEDICATIONS

Depending on the patient, a health-care professional may prescribe psychotropic medications (medications that change brain function) to be taken along with or without therapy sessions. Dozens of medications are available to treat mental health conditions such as depression and bipolar disorder. While doctors may have a general idea of what medication will be effective for a particular person, no one can predict which options will work best. Doctors and patients discuss the benefits and potential risks before making a decision about which medication to use.

Often, starting a new medication is a process of trial and error. Patients and their doctors must work together to find the medication that gives the best result with the fewest side effects. A medication may take up to three months to achieve its full effect, and patients may be on psychotropic medications for several months or longer. If the patient does not feel better after that time, the doctor may add or substitute another antidepressant or try another type of medication. For example, a person with bipolar disorder such as Michelle Prichard may need an antidepressant, a mood stabilizer, and an antipsychotic medication. Bipolar patients taking only antidepressants may be at risk of cycling into manic episodes.

Commonly used psychotropic medications include the following:

- Antidepressants (such as Prozac, Zoloft, Wellbutrin, and Cymbalta) help treat depression by influencing the brain chemicals serotonin, dopamine, and norepinephrine, which are associated with regulation of emotions.

- Mood stabilizers (various forms of lithium) reduce the mood swings of bipolar disorder.

- Antianxiety medications (such as Xanax, Tranxene, and Valium) reduce emotional and physical symptoms of anxiety.

- Anticonvulsants (such as Tegretol and Lamictal), normally used to treat seizures, also work as mood stabilizers in some people.

- Antipsychotics (such as Abilify and Latuda), originally developed to treat conditions involving psychosis, such as schizophrenia, are also sometimes used to treat acute mania, bipolar disorder, and persistent depression.

Psychotropic medication can cause serious side effects, especially in some children, adolescents, and young adults. These can include increased anxiety, agitation, irritability, anger, and even suicidal thoughts, especially among younger people (although studies show no link between such thoughts and increased suicide attempts.) Patients and their families must immediately notify their doctors if they notice any of these symptoms. Doctors can assess the situation and work with families to make adjustments to the type or amount of medication a patient is taking.

INTENSIVE AND LONG-TERM TREATMENT PROGRAMS

People with mental health conditions and substance abuse problems who need more intensive help may enter day treatment or partial hospitalization programs. These programs generally last several weeks, with patients spending several hours a day at a facility where they regularly meet with mental health professionals and other patients for therapy and to discuss medication. Some people may voluntarily enter inpatient psychiatric hospitals or substance abuse treatment centers. These patients may choose to leave at any time. However, when someone is in an acute crisis in which they risk injuring themselves or other people—as Paul Pope was in 2014—police can take this person to a hospital, where a doctor may admit him or her to a psychiatric facility. In an involuntary hold, in which the patient does not agree to the admission, a patient is admitted to a hospital for seventy-two hours for assessment by experts. Psychiatrists decide if further inpatient hospitalization is warranted. Inpatient hospitalization provides continuous care in a safe environment. It may be necessary for people who are suicidal or so severely affected by mental illness that they cannot function.

A residential treatment facility, where patients live for weeks, months, or even years while receiving treatment, provides a more homelike setting than does a psychiatric hospital. Admissions may be voluntary, although sometimes they are mandated by a judge (perhaps for nonviolent crimes, long-standing drug abuse, or being a danger to self or others). Constant meetings and therapy with mental health professionals and interaction with peers and staff over several months can go a long way toward resolving patients' problems. Kendra Pope says her son Paul is making great progress in the residential treatment facility where he currently lives.

MANY PATHS TO RECOVERY

Because everyone is unique, a certain treatment may help one person but not another. Through trial and error, Michelle Prichard and her physicians eventually found a combination of medications that helped her control her bipolar disorder. "It took several years for the doctors to come up with the right 'cocktail' of medications," she notes. "I'm on lithium, Abilify, Lamictal, and Prozac. They work very well for me."

While medication can be a crucial tool to help fight mental illness and suicidal thoughts, most people struggling to avoid suicide still face a complicated path to recovery—one that requires perseverance, patience, and honesty with themselves and others. Amanda Lipp, mental health consultant, speaks publicly about the many issues that drove her to a suicide attempt in her teens. "I was in therapy and on medication the last two years of high school," Amanda says, "yet I still had a breakdown my freshman year of college resulting in psychiatric hospitalization." Treatment did not resolve her issues overnight but laid the foundation on which she was able to build a stable, fulfilling life.

BARRIERS TO TREATMENT

Despite the wide variety of mental health treatment options available, statistics show that only three out of ten people who have died by suicide received mental health care in the year before they died. Many people with mental health issues receive no treatment at all. Why don't more people get help for mental health problems? According to a 2013 WHO survey, the two most common reasons people give for not seeking treatment are the belief that they do not need treatment and that they wish to handle the problem themselves. Other reasons include a belief that the problem is not severe, the hope that it will get better by itself, an inability to afford medical care, the belief that mental health care does not work, and a lack of available providers.

> "I felt so helpless and lost in myself, like nothing or nobody could help. If I couldn't even help myself, how in the world could anybody else help me?"
>
> —Amanda Lipp, speaking of her severe depression

Stigma is another reason people may not seek help for their

problems. Encountering negative and false perceptions of mental illness in popular culture or among friends and family members can discourage someone from acknowledging that they are struggling with mental health issues. "The stigma of depression is that it comes with the sense that you shouldn't have it to begin with," says author Libba Bray, who lives with depression. "That it is self-indulgence or emotional incompetence rather than actual illness. This brings on attendant feelings of shame and self-loathing, which only exacerbate the pain, isolation, and hopelessness of the condition."

Amanda Lipp says that she worked to overcome societal stigma against mental illness by changing the way she viewed herself. "When I started to acknowledge my identity as a person, and to see adverse experiences as *opportunities* to grow and diversify, I noticed a change within myself and how others viewed me. People started to treat me in the same way I had evolved to view myself—with respect and pride. It's easier said than done, but with support, this reverses the cycle of stigma and cultivates empathy. This process is contagious."

While hospitalized after a psychotic breakdown her first year of college, mental health activist Amanda Lipp created a unique form of crayon art as a way to express her feelings and find beauty amidst pain.

SUICIDE: MYTH OR FACT?

Stereotypes and misconceptions about suicide can put people who are already suffering severe distress or mental illness into dangerously narrowed pigeonholes. According to the American Foundation for Suicide Prevention, common myths about suicide include these:

- **Myth:** People who take their own lives are selfish, cowardly, or just looking for attention.
- **Fact:** People who attempt suicide are in pain and need help. More than 90 percent of people who die by suicide have at least one treatable mental illness such as depression, anxiety, bipolar disorder, schizophrenia, or substance abuse. With better recognition and treatment, many suicides can be prevented.

- **Myth:** Someone making suicidal threats won't really do it.
- **Fact:** Those who talk about committing suicide or express thoughts about wanting to die are at risk and need attention and help. Most people who die by suicide give some indication or warning beforehand. Take all threats of suicide seriously. They are a cry for help.

- **Myth:** You can't prevent a suicide. Nothing can stop people from taking their own lives if they want to.
- **Fact:** Most people who think about suicide really don't want to die. They are looking for a way to stop their emotional and physical pain. You can help to prevent suicide. Intervention works. Treatment helps.

- **Myth:** Asking a person if he is thinking about suicide will put the thought in his head and prompt him to try it.
- **Fact:** If you know a person is depressed or in a crisis, asking him if he's thinking about suicide is actually helpful. Realizing that someone cares enough to ask gives him a chance to talk about his struggles. That conversation can be the first step toward finding help and solutions.

- **Myth:** Suicide prevention efforts such as locking up guns and adding barriers on bridges to prevent jumping won't reduce suicides. People will find another way.
- **Fact:** Many suicides are impulsive. Limiting access to means of suicide can prevent someone from acting in response to a moment

of crisis. This provides time for the person to change her mind, time to resolve the crisis, and time for her family and friends to intervene. Even an hour or two can make the difference between living and dying.

- **Myth:** Medications and therapy are of little help.
- **Fact:** Treatment *can* work, whether it comes in the form of therapy, the right medication, or a combination of methods. Helping people get treatment for mental illness or substance abuse greatly reduces their risk for suicide. Finding the best treatments may take time, but it can save lives.

HELPING OTHERS AVOID SUICIDE

Between one half and three-fourths of people who think about taking their own lives tell someone about their thoughts, feelings, and plans in advance. Even more often, friends may notice unusual behavior or worrisome comments, such as, "I hate my life" or "I won't be around to bother you much longer." A friend may give away her favorite possessions. He may cancel plans and stay home alone. A teen who suspects that a friend is thinking about suicide can ask directly, "Are you thinking about suicide? Do you have a plan to hurt yourself?" Experts say asking these questions will not push a person toward suicide. On the contrary, if a person is already thinking about suicide, talking about suicidal thoughts is a helpful and necessary step toward preventing suicide.

One suicide prevention organization offers tips on how to talk to a person who is thinking about suicide:

- Be yourself. Don't worry about finding the right words. Your voice, expression, and attitude will show that you care.
- Listen. Let your friend freely express despair and anger. Assure your friend that she is doing the right thing by talking about her feelings. Even a negative conversation is better than no conversation.

- Be patient, calm, and accepting. Don't judge or criticize your friend's actions or feelings. Don't try to reason with your friend or argue with his perception of himself or the world. Don't give advice that your friend hasn't asked for. You don't have to be your friend's therapist. You just need to help him open up.
- Offer hope. Assure your friend that help is available. Let her know she's important to you and to others.
- Don't promise *not* to tell. If your friend's life is at stake, you must tell an adult who can help him.

Therapist Chris Crutcher says, "Suicide is often impulsive with kids. If we can catch them at the time they're ready to do it, we can often stop future attempts." If a teen is worried that a friend may attempt suicide very soon, it is crucial not to leave the person alone. Stay with the person and contact an adult. If no adult is available and the danger is immediate, call a suicide prevention hotline. In an extreme case, when someone already has access to a means of suicide and either has used it or is about to use it, call 911 for immediate assistance.

How else can teens help prevent friends or family members from taking their own lives? "They can offer support," Chris Crutcher says. "Though I would counsel them on recognized warning signs, I would also tell them in some cases, there's no way to tell who is thinking about suicide. Be kind and inclusive. That's the mantra. And you don't have to be cheesy or a goody-goody to pull that off."

e.E. Charlton-Trujillo agrees that kindness is a vital part of suicide prevention. "Being kinder starts by accepting others for whatever weird-beautiful, strange-ordinary, athletic-nerdy versions of themselves they may be," she says. "We gotta get past this notion that being different is somehow bad. Each of us comes into this world with imperfections that make us unique and interesting and attractive. To be kinder, change the way we look at each other. It's about redefining the cool. Weird is the new cool!"

ActiveMinds Inc., a group that works toward suicide prevention among college students, organized this display of hundreds of backpacks in New York City in April 2012. The group displayed a total of 1,100 backpacks in various locations to represent the 1,000 college students who commit suicide each year.

HELP IS HERE

Reaching out for help can make a world of difference for teens considering suicide. Family, friends, and other adults are willing and able to help. Kendra Pope, whose family weathered her son Paul's suicide attempt, says, "I would tell anyone considering suicide there really is hope. There are people who can help you and you need to reach out to them. Get a mentor as soon as possible, someone you can call anytime to help you deal with your stressors. Find a safe person to talk to, a sounding board. Know that people care. Family and friends want to help. You only have to reach out and ask."

Fourteen-year-old Mattea Landon echoes that sentiment. "Get help," she says. "I lost a piece of my heart the day that Uncle Jesse died. I remember it all: the funeral, the depression, the sorrow each year on his birthday when my mom says how old he would be if he'd lived. If this ever happens to you, DON'T try to bottle up the pain. It only makes you feel like an emotional wreck. Prevent yourself from sinking into too much depression. Don't do what my uncle did. Trust me, you would be terribly missed."

BY THE NUMBERS

- About 80 to 90 percent of people who seek treatment for depression improve with therapy, medication, or both.
- Only half of all Americans experiencing an episode of major depression receive treatment.
- Between 50 and 75 percent of people who attempt suicide talk to others about their suicidal thoughts and plans in advance.

SOURCE NOTES

6 Susan Caldwell, interview with the author, February 26, 2015.

8 "Definitions: Self-Directed Violence." Centers for Disease Control and Prevention. http://www.cdc.gov/violenceprevention/suicide/definitions.html. Accessed November 5, 2015.

9 Arrington, *Aftershock: Help, Hope, and Healing in the Wake of Suicide*. Nashville, TN: B&H Publishing Group, 2003, p 1.

9 "Shock." *Alliance of Hope for Suicide Survivors*. August 2011. http://www.allianceofhope.org/survivor_experience/2011/08/shock.html#more

10 "Sadness, Depression and Despair." *Alliance of Hope for Suicide Survivors*. August 2011. http://www.allianceofhope.org/survivor_experience/2011/08/sadness-depression-and-despair.html#more

10 "Anger." *Alliance of Hope for Suicide Survivors*. August 2011. http://www.allianceofhope.org/survivor_experience/2011/08/anger.html#more

10 "Anger." *Alliance of Hope for Suicide Survivors*. August 2011. http://www.allianceofhope.org/survivor_experience/2011/08/anger.html#more

10 Candy Neely Arrington, *Aftershock: Help, Hope, and Healing in the Wake of Suicide*. Nashville, TN: B&H Publishing Group, 2003, p 42.

11 Kitty Workman, interviews with the author, September 24, 2014 and March 4, 2015.

11 Domenica Di Piazza, interview with the author. March 2, 2015.

11 Maria Mercedes Lara, "Zelda Williams Shares Message About Depression One Year After Dad Robin Williams's Death: 'Hold onto the Possibility of Hope." *People*. http://www.people.com/article/zelda-williams-robin-williams-depression-instagram

11 Patti Zarling, "Son's Suicide Freezes Time for De Pere Mom." *Green Bay Press Gazette*. 8/29/14. http://www.greenbaypressgazette.com/story/news/local/2014/08/28/sons-suicide-freezes-time-mom/14741477. Accessed May 28, 2015.

13 Domenica Di Piazza, interview with the author. March 2, 2015.

13 Chris Crutcher, interview with the author, March 3, 2015.

14 Susan Caldwell, interview with the author, February 26, 2015.

14 Community Forum. *Alliance of Hope for Suicide Survivors*. http://www.allianceofhope.org/alliance-of-hope-for-suic/community-forum.html. Accessed May 28, 2015.

17 "Religion and Suicide." *Religion & Ethnics Newsweekly*. October 21, 2005. http://www.pbs.org/wnet/religionandethics/2005/10/21/october-21-2005-religion-and-suicide/11870.

18 Heather Landon, interview with the author, October 12, 2014.

20 Jeanne Miller, personal interview with the author, February 15, 2015.

20 "Preventing Suicide: A Global Imperative." World Health Organization. http://www.who.int/mental_health/suicide-prevention/world_report_2014/en. Accessed May 28, 2015.

21 "Preventing Suicide: A Global Imperative." World Health Organization. http://www.who.int/mental_health/suicide-prevention/world_report_2014/en. Accessed May 28, 2015.

21 "Preventing Suicide: A Global Imperative." World Health Organization. http://www.who.int/mental_health/suicide-prevention/world_report_2014/en. Accessed May 28, 2015.

23 Lenny Bernstein and Lena H. Sun, "Robin Williams in a Group Facing Higher Risk of Suicide: Older White Men with Depression." *The Washington Post*. August 12, 2014. https://www.washingtonpost.com/national/health-science/robin-williams-in-a-group-facing-higher-risk-of-suicide-older-white-men-with-depression/2014/08/12/8e1164d6-225e-11e4-86ca-6f03cbd15c1a_story.html

23 Tavernise, Sabrina. "Rise in Suicide by Black Children Surprises Researchers." *The New York Times*. May 18, 2015. http://www.nytimes.com/2015/05/19/health/suicide-rate-for-black-children-surged-in-2-decades-study-says.html?_r=0.

24 Tony Dokoupil, "Why Suicide Has Become an Epidemic—and What We Can Do to Help." *Newsweek*. May 22, 2013. http://www.newsweek.com/2013/05/22/why-suicide-has-become-epidemic-and-what-we-can-do-help-237434.html. Accessed May 28, 2015.

26 Sharon Hong, "In Studying Suicide, He Shines a Light on a Secret Shame." *UCLA Newsroom*. September 26, 2014. http://newsroom.ucla.edu/stories/in-studying-suicide-he-shines-a-light-on-a-secret-shame. February 18, 2015.

26 William Styron, *Darkness Visible: a Memoir of Madness*. New York, NY: Random House, 1990.

27 William Styron, *Darkness Visible: a Memoir of Madness*. New York, NY: Random House, 1990.

28 Libba Bray, "Miles and Miles of No-Man's Land." *Libby Bray*. March 2, 2014. https://libbabray.wordpress.com/2014/03/02/miles-and-miles-of-no-mans-land. Used with permission given in email with author (slightly revised). Accessed May 28, 2015.

28 "Step Inside My Head: Teens Speak Out On Mental Health." *Active Minds*. August 14, 2012. http://activeminds.org/our-programming/step-inside-my-head.

29 Michelle Prichard, personal interview with the author, February 19, 2015.

29 Kevin Hines, *Cracked, Not Broken: Surviving and Thriving After a Suicide*. Lanham, MD: Rowman & Littlefield Publishers. 2013. P. 57.

31 Hal Arkowitz and Scott Lilienfeld. "Is Depression Just Bad Chemistry?" *Scientific American*. March 1, 2014. http://www.scientificAmerican.com/article/is-depression-just-bad-chemistry. Accessed August 15, 2015.

31 Alix Spiegel, "When it Comes to Depression, Serotonin isn't the Whole Story." *National Public Radio*. January 23, 2014. http://www.npr.org/blogs/health/2012/01/23/145525853/when-it-comes-to-depression-serotonin-isnt-the-whole-story. Accessed May 28, 2015.

32 Carolyn C. Ross, "Suicide: One of Addiction's Hidden Risks." *Psychology Today*. February 20, 2014. http://www.psychologytoday.com/blog/real-healing/201402/suicide-one-addiction-s-hidden-risks. Accessed February 19, 2015.

33 Carolyn C. Ross, "Suicide: One of Addiction's Hidden Risks." *Psychology Today*. February 20, 2014. http://www.psychologytoday.com/blog/real-healing/201402/suicide-one-addiction-s-hidden-risks. Accessed February 19, 2015.

35 e.E. Charlton-Trujillo, personal interview with author. December 16, 2014.

35 Kitty Workman, personal interviews with the author, September 24, 2014 and March 4, 2015.

36 Robert Glatter, "Genetic Biomarker Identified That May Predict Suicide Risk." *Forbes*. August 9, 2014. http://www.forbes.com/sites/robertglatter/2014/08/09/genetic-biomarker-identified-that-may-predict-suicide-risk/print.

40 Carlie Madison, interview with author. February 23, 2015.

42 Amanda Lipp, interviews with author September 26, 2014 to June 11, 2015.

42 "Transgender teen cites family bullying in suicide note: #HisNameWasZander." *LGBTQ Nation*. February 19, 2015. http://www.lgbtqnation.com/2015/02/transgender-teen-cites-family-bullying-in-suicide-note-hisnamewaszander. Accessed May 28, 2015.

43 Amanda Lipp, interviews with author September 26, 2014 to June 11, 2015.

44 Davis Evans, interview with author, October 24, 2014.

45 Davis Evans, interview with author, October 24, 2014.

46 Alexis O., "Ending Unhealthy Relationships." love is respect.org. October 16, 14. http://www.loveisrespect.org/content/ending-unhealthy-relationships. Accessed May 28, 2015.

49 Allen Pierleoni, "Mother of Bullying Victim Strikes Back with Efforts to Save Others." *Sacramento Bee*. August 21, 2013. http://www.sacbee.com/entertainment/living/family/article2576715.html. August 15, 2015.

49 "Lisa Ford-Berry, bullying, and losing her son to suicide." YouTube. April 19, 2013. Posted April 22, 2013. https://www.youtube.com/watch?v=PRyGY_EsPLI

49 Allen Pierleoni, "Mother of Bullying Victim Strikes Back with Efforts to Save Others." Sacramento Bee. August 21, 2013. http://www.sacbee.com/entertainment/living/family/article2576715.html. August 15, 2015.

50 "The Relationship Between Bullying and Suicide." Center for Disease Control. 2014. http://www.cdc.gov/violenceprevention/pdf/bullying-suicide-translation-final-a.pdf. Accessed May 28, 2015.

50 e.E. Charlton-Trujillo, interview with author, December 16, 2014.

52 e.E. Charlton-Trujillo, interview with author, December 16, 2014.

52 Laurette Gaberman, interview with author, May 9, 2015.

53 Susan Caldwell, interview with the author, February 26, 2015.

53 Meggie Royer, "The Morning I Killed Myself." *Writings for Winter*. July 31, 2015. http://writingsforwinter.tumblr.com/post/125560163524/the-morning-after-i-killed-myself. Used with permission. 8/28/15.

56 James Swift, "Roswell mother fights for VA changes following son's death." *Neighbor Newspapers*. July 23, 2014. http://www.neighbornewspapers.com/view/full_story/25482743/article-Roswell-mother-fights-for-VA-changes-following-son-s-death. October 7, 2015.

57 "The Big Lie: Why 22 Veteran Suicides a Day is False." *Military Suicide Report*. September 29, 2014. https://themilitarysuicidereport.wordpress.com/2014/09/29/the-big-lie-why-22-veteran-suicides-a-day-is-false/. Accessed May 28, 2015.

58 Caleb S. Cage, interviews with author. October 15, 2014 and May 5, 2015.

59 Alan Zarembo, "Suicide Rate of Female Military Veterans is Called Staggering." *Los Angeles Times*. June 8, 2015. http://www.latimes.com/nation/la-na-female-veteran-suicide-20150608-story.html#page=1. Accessed June 8, 2015.

59 Gregg Zoroya, "40,000 Suicides Annually, Yet America Simply Shrugs." *USA Today*. http://www.usatoday.com/story/news/nation/2014/10/09/suicide-mental-health-prevention-research/15276353.

61 Timothy Hale, "Searching for Answers: A Panel Review of Army Reserve Suicides." Defense Video & Imagery Distribution System. September 2, 2014. https://www.dvidshub.net/news/140976/searching-answers-panel-review-army-reserve-suicides#.VP4ne_nF_Tp. Accessed May 28, 2015.

62 Sharon Jayson, "Suicide Risk Among Soldiers May be Rooted in their Past." *USA Today*. August 9, 2014. http://www.usatoday.com/story/news/nation/2014/08/09/military-suicide-childhood-trauma/13818841. Accessed May 28, 2015.

62 Yochi Dreazen, "Five Myths about Military Suicides." *The Washingon Post*.
November 7, 2014. http://www.washingtonpost.com/opinions/five-myths-about-
suicide-in-the-military/2014/11/07/61ceb0aa-637b-11e4-836c-83bc4f26eb67_
story.html. Accessed May 28, 2015.

64 Gilreath, Tamika D. and Stephani L. Wrabel, Katherine S. Sullivan, Gordon
P. Capp, Ilan Roziner, Rami Benbenishty, Ron A. Astor. "Suicidality Among
Military-Connected Adolescents in California Schools." SpringerLink. http://link.
springer.com/article/10.1007/s00787-015-0696-2.

64 Caleb S. Cage, interviews with author. October 15, 2014 and May 5, 2015.

66 Kimberly Leonard, "Obama Signs Suicide Prevention Bill to Aid Veterans."
US News & World Report. February 12, 2015. http://www.usnews.com/news/
articles/2015/02/12/obama-signs-veterans-suicide-prevention-bill

66 Jenna Brayton. "The Clay Hunt Act: What the President Just Signed." The White
House. February 12, 2015. https://www.whitehouse.gov/blog/2015/02/12/clay-
hunt-act-what-president-just-signed.

67 Caleb S. Cage, interviews with author. October 15, 2014 and May 5, 2015.

67 Sarah Childress. "Why Soldiers Keep Losing to Suicide." *Frontline*. PBS.
December 20, 2012 http://www.pbs.org/wgbh/pages/frontline/foreign-affairs-
defense/why-soldiers-keep-losing-to-suicide. Accessed May 28, 2015.

68 Lynn Jolicoeur, "National Guard Struggles to Combat High Suicide Rate."
WBUR: an NPR station. September 18, 2014. http://www.wbur.org/2014/09/18/
massachusetts-national-guard-suicide. Accessed May 28, 2015.

70 Domenica Di Piazza, interview with author, March 2, 2015.

70 Lenny Bernstein and Lena H. Sun. "Robin Williams in a Group Facing Higher
Risk of Suicide: Older White Men with Depression." *The Washington Post*.
August 12, 2014. http://www.washingtonpost.com/national/health-science/
robin-williams-in-a-group-facing higher-risk-of-suicide-older-white-men-with-
depression/2014/08/12/8e1164d6-225e-11e4-86ca-6f03cbd15c1a_story.html.
Accessed May 28, 2015.

72 Jeremy Hobson, "Suicide-proofing the Golden Gate Bridge," *National Public
Radio*. July 7, 2014. http://hereandnow.wbur.org/2014/07/07/suicide-nets-golden-
gate-bridge. Accessed April 10, 2015.

72 Lydia O'Connor, "A New Feature on the Golden Gate Bridge Could Save
Hundreds of Lives a Year," *Huffington Post*. December 29, 2014. http://
www.huffingtonpost.com/2014/12/29/golden-gate-bridge-suicide-barrier-
design_n_6374712.html. Accessed May 28, 2015.

73 Katherine A. Hempstead, Julie A. Phillips. "Rising Suicide Among Adults Aged
40–64 Years." *American Journal of Preventive Medicine*, 2015; DOI: 10.1016/j.
amepre.2014.11.006. Accessed May 28, 2015.

74 Kerri Wagner, interview with author. April 2, 2015.

74 Kerri Wagner, interview with author, April 2, 2015.

75 Nicole Weisensee Eagan, "Terminally Ill Woman Brittany Maynard has Ended Her Own Life." *People*. November 2, 2014. http://www.people.com/article/brittany-maynard-died-terminal-brain-cancer. Accessed May 28, 2015.

75 Michael Muskal, "Brittany Maynard Dead; Right to Die Widely Supported and Widely Illegal." *Los Angeles Times*. November 4, 2014. http://www.latimes.com/nation/nationnow/la-na-brittany-maynard-right-to-die-20141103-story.html. Accessed May 28, 2015.

77 Nick Visser, "Stephen Hawking Says He Would Consider Assisted Suicide If He Had 'Nothing More To Contribute.'" *The Huffington Post*. June 3, 2015. http://www.huffingtonpost.com/2015/06/03/stephen-hawking-assisted-suicide_n_7502598.html. Accessed June 3, 2015.

77 Susan Donaldson James, "Jack Kevorkian Dies, Leaves Controversial Legacy, No Successor." *ABC News*. June 3, 2011. http://abcnews.go.com/Health/jack-kevorkian-godfather-die-movement-leaves-controversial-legacy/story?id=13752603.

78 "Californians Against Assisted Suicide Response to AB2x15 Passage by the California State Senate." *Californians Against Assisted Suicide*. September 11, 2015. http://noassistedsuicideca.org/item/382-californians-against-assisted-suicide-response-to-ab2x15-passage-by-the-california-state-senate.

81 Kendra Pope, interview with author, April 13, 2015.

83 Ann Steiner, PhD, interview with author, May 6, 2015.

84 Chris Crutcher, interview with author, March 3, 2015.

85 *A New State of Mind: Ending the Stigma of Mental Illness*. 6:00. KVIE Public Television. April 5, 2013. http://vids.kvie.org/video/2365021031. Accessed May 28, 2015.

88 Michelle Prichard, interview with author, February 19, 2015.

88 Amanda Lipp, interviews with author September 26, 2014 to June 11, 2015.

88 Amanda Lipp, interviews with author September 26, 2014 to June 11, 2015.

89 Libba Bray, "Miles and Miles of No-Man's Land." *Libba Bray*. March 2, 2014. https://libbabray.wordpress.com/2014/03/02/miles-and-miles-of-no-mans-land/. Used with permission given in email with author, April 26, 2015.

89 Amanda Lipp, interviews with author September 26, 2014 to June 11, 2015.

90 "Understanding Suicide: Myth vs. Fact." *American Foundation for Suicide Prevention*. September 6, 2013. https://www.afsp.org/news-events/in-the-news/understanding-suicide-myth-vs.-fact.

91 "Suicide Prevention: How to Help Someone Who Is Suicidal." *HelpGuide.org*. http://www.helpguide.org/articles/suicide-prevention/suicide-prevention-helping-someone-who-is-suicidal.htm#tip1

92 Chris Crutcher, interview with author, March 3, 2015.

92 Chris Crutcher, interview with author, March 3, 2015.

92 e.E. Charlton-Trujillo, interview with author, December 16, 2014.

94 Kendra Pope, interview with author, April 13, 2015.

94 Mattea Landon, interview with author, October 14, 2014.

GLOSSARY

antianxiety medication: medication used to treat anxiety disorder, a state of extreme nervousness or worry

anticonvulsants: medications most often used to control seizures. In some cases, they help stabilize moods in people with bipolar disorder.

antidepressants: medications that affect the brain chemicals serotonin, dopamine, and norepinephrine used to help reduce the lows associated with depression

antipsychotics: medications used to treat several mental illnesses, including acute mania, bipolar disorder, and persistent depression

bipolar disorder: a serious mental condition that results in alternating periods of depression and elation, or mania. Bipolar is sometimes called manic-depressive disorder.

bullying: aggressive behavior toward another person that is intended to belittle that person through lies, threats, and physical or verbal attack

cutting: the purposeful cutting of oneself with sharp objects such as knives and razors. This form of self-harm is used to control emotional pain by redirecting it to a physical sensation.

cyberbullying: bullying through electronic media such as text messages, e-mails, or social networking sites. This type of bullying typically includes posting fake profiles, embarrassing photos, or videos. It can also involve spreading lies or embarrassing information about another person.

dating violence: see domestic violence

day treatment program: a type of intensive outpatient treatment program to help a person deal with mental health and substance abuse issues. The program involves several hours a day at a clinic or facility in which a patient will have therapy and talk to peers in a safe environment.

Department of Veterans Affairs (VA): the government agency in charge of managing health care for all US veterans. The agency manages more than 1,700 hospitals, clinics, community living centers, counseling centers, and other facilities.

depression: a persistent feeling of sadness and unhappiness so severe that it interferes with normal activities. The feeling may last weeks, months, or even years and can affect every aspect of life.

domestic violence: the purposeful use of threats, assault, and other verbal or physical abuse to control another person. Domestic violence occurs between two people in a close relationship and can include family members and dating partners.

group therapy: a type of psychotherapy in which one or more therapists work with several people at the same time in the same setting.

mood stabilizer: medications that help even out the mood cycling between mania and depression. They are often prescribed for patients with bipolar disorder.

National Suicide Prevention Lifeline: this hotline provides free and confidential support to people in suicidal crisis and any other type of emotional distress twenty-four hours a day and seven days a week (1-800-273-8255)

neurotransmitters: natural brain chemicals such as dopamine, norepinephrine, and serotonin that send signals between nerve cells. Scientists believe these chemicals influence mood, mental health, and behavior.

physician-assisted suicide: a death in which a physician aids a patient's death by providing information about the means to do so to a patient, knowing the patient may commit suicide.

post-traumatic stress disorder (PTSD): a mental health condition triggered by a terrifying event, such as war experiences, accidents, or other trauma. PTSD can include frightening flashbacks, nightmares, and anxiety and is often linked with traumatic brain injury.

psychiatrist: a medical doctor (MD) with specialized training in psychiatry, the diagnosing and treatment of mental health conditions. A psychiatrist can legally prescribe medications and may also provide assistance through talk therapy.

psychologist: a mental health specialist (PhD) with extensive training in diagnosing and treating mental health conditions. Most psychologists cannot legally prescribe medications.

residential treatment facility: a live-in health-care facility that provides a homelike setting for treatment of mental illness or substance abuse among residents. The facility is sometimes referred to as rehabilitation or rehab.

stigma: a mark of shame or disgrace associated with a particular condition or circumstance. Mental illness and suicide carry social stigma in the United States.

substance abuse: the purposeful misuse of potentially harmful substances such as alcohol, illegal drugs, and nonmedical use of prescription medications, such as sedatives and pain medications. These substances are typically used to alter a person's perception of reality so as to relieve stress, depression, anxiety, or pain.

suicide: a death caused by an action taken with the intention to die

suicide attempt: taking action with intention to die. A suicide attempt may or may not result in injury.

suicide ideation: thinking about committing suicide or making a suicide plan

talk therapy: a form of mental health assessment and treatment that involves conversation between a therapist and a client about mental health conditions such as depression and anxiety. Trained therapists include appropriately licensed social workers, mental health nurse practitioners, psychologists, and psychiatrists.

traumatic brain injury (TBI): injuries to the brain caused by blows to the head (as in sports), penetrating objects (such as bullets), or blast jury (caused by pressure waves traveling through the brain faster than the speed of sound such as those created by a bomb blast)

SELECTED BIBLIOGRAPHY

"About Teen Suicide." Nemours. Accessed May 27, 2015. http://kidshealth.org/parent/emotions/behavior/suicide.html#.

Arkowitz, Hal, and Scott Lilienfeld. "Is Depression Just Bad Chemistry?" *Scientific American*, March 1, 2014. http://www.scientificAmerican.com/article/is-depression-just-bad-chemistry/.

Cox, David, and Candy Arrington. *Aftershock: Help, Hope, and Healing in the Wake of Suicide*. Nashville: B&H, 2003.

"Cyberbullying." Stop Bullying.gov. Accessed May 27, 2015. http://www.stopbullying.gov/cyberbullying/index.html.

Dokoupil, Tony. "Why Suicide Has Become an Epidemic—and What We Can Do to Help." *Newsweek*, May 23, 2013. http://www.newsweek.com/2013/05/22/why-suicide-has-become-epidemic-and-what-we-can-do-help-237434.html.

"Facts about Bullying." Stop Bullying.gov. Accessed May 27, 2015. http://www.stopbullying.gov/news/media/facts/#listing.

"Facts and Figures." American Foundation for Suicide Prevention. Accessed May 27, 2015. https://www.afsp.org/understanding-suicide/facts-and-figures.

Grant, Jaime M., Lisa A. Mottet, and Justin Tanis. With Jack Harrison, Jody L. Herman, and Mara Keisling. "Injustice at Every Turn: Report of the National Transgender Discrimination Survey." National Center for Transgender Equality. Accessed May 27, 2015. http://www.thetaskforce.org/static_html/downloads/reports/reports/ntds_full.pdf.

Hale, Timothy. "Searching for Answers: A Panel Review of Army Reserve Suicides." Defense Video & Imagery Distribution System. September 2, 2014. https://www.dvidshub.net/news/140976/searching-answers-panel-review-army-reserve-suicides#.VWZCCU_BwXC.

"Preventing Suicide: A Global Imperative." World Health Organization. Accessed May 27, 2015. http://www.who.int/mental_health/suicide-prevention/world_report_2014/en/.

Styron, William. *Darkness Visible: A Memoir of Madness*. New York: Random House, 1990.

"Substance Use and Mental Health Estimates from the 2013 National Survey on Drug Use and Health." Substance Abuse and Mental Health Services Administration. Accessed May 27, 2015. http://beta.samhsa.gov/data/sites/default/files/NSDUH-SR200-RecoveryMonth-2014/NSDUH-SR200-RecoveryMonth-2014.htm.

"Suicide Prevention." Substance Abuse and Mental Health Services Administration. Accessed May 27, 2015. http://www.samhsa.gov/suicide-prevention.

"Surviving a Suicide Loss: A Resource and Healing Guide." American Foundation for Suicide Prevention. Accessed May 27, 2015. https://www.afsp.org/coping-with-suicide-loss/where-do-i-begin/resource-and-healing-guide.

"The Survivor Experience." Alliance of Hope for Suicide Loss Survivors. Accessed May 27, 2015. http://www.allianceofhope.org/survivor_experience.

"Understanding the Connection between Suicide and Substance Abuse." Substance Abuse and Mental health Services Administration. Accessed May 27, 2015. https://captus.samhsa.gov/sites/default/files/suicide_webinar1_transcript_final_2_ll_09-19-14_0.pdf.

"USA Suicide: 2013 Official Final Data." American Association of Suicidology. Accessed May 27, 2015. http://www.suicidology.org/Portals/14/docs/Resources/FactSheets/2013datapgsv3.pdf.

Zoroya, Gregg. "40,000 Suicides Annually, Yet America Simply Shrugs." *USA Today*, October 10, 2014. http://www.usatoday.com/longform/news/nation/2014/10/09/suicide-mental-health-prevention-research/15276353.

FURTHER INFORMATION

Books

Charlton-Trujillo, e.E. *Fat Angie*. Somerville, MA: Candlewick, 2013. This novel tells the story of Angie—a fat, bullied, and desperate teen. The entire school starts tormenting Angie after she tries but fails to kill herself at a basketball game. Her sister's absence (as a possible prisoner of war in Iraq) adds to Angie's misery. Ultimately, Angie triumphs over her challenges.

Goldsmith, Connie. *Traumatic Brain Injury: From Concussion to Coma*. Minneapolis: Twenty-First Century Books, 2014. Learn about traumatic brain injury and post-traumatic stress disorder in the chapter about the military and how they may contribute to mental health issues, including suicide.

Hines, Kevin. *Cracked, Not Broken: Surviving and Thriving after a Suicide Attempt*. Lanham, MD: Rowman & Littlefield, 2013. Hines, one of the few people to survive a jump off the Golden Gate Bridge, tells his story from teen depression and substance abuse to his suicide attempt to nationally recognized suicide prevention advocate and public speaker. He stresses that recovery is a lifelong process but one that is well worth pursuing.

Hopkins, Ellen. *Rumble*. New York: Margaret K. McElderry Books, 2014. In this novel, Matt blames himself—and others—when his younger brother Luke takes his own life after relentless bullying.

Letran, Jacqui. *I Would, but My DAMN MIND Won't Let Me: A Teen Girl's Guide to Understanding and Controlling Her Thoughts and Feelings*. Seattle, WA: CreateSpace, 2015. Written by a nurse practitioner, this book offers tips and strategies to help girls combat depression and overcome negative thoughts to create the life they want and deserve.

Mayrok, Aija. *The Survival Guide to Bullying: Written by a Teen for a Teen*. New York: Scholastic, 2015. Originally self-published by this teen author who was bullied, the book talks about how to survive bullying from a teen's point of view.

Moragne, Wendy. *Depression*. USA Today Health Reports: Diseases and Disorders series. Minneapolis: Twenty-First Century Books, 2011. Learn more about depression and how it can be treated.

Pedrick, Cherry, and Bruce Hyman. *Anxiety Disorders*. USA Today Health Reports: Diseases and Disorders series. Minneapolis: Twenty-First Century Books, 2012. Learn about anxiety and how it can be treated.

Ramey, Stacie. *The Sister Pact*. Naperville, IL: Sourcebooks, 2015. This young adult novel tells the story of two sisters who vow to take their lives together. Told from the perspective of the sister who lives, the teen spirals into grief, prescription pill abuse, and mysterious visions, which lead her to uncover unexpected secrets.

Stork, Francisco X. *The Memory of Light*. New York: Arthur A. Levine, 2016. Vicky Cruz and three other teens bond and learn to live with depression and mental illness. This novel offers dazzling insight into their journey as they return from the darkness together.

Video and Audio Resources

Break the Silence: Stop the Violence. Centers for Control and Prevention. 4:12. Released August 4, 2008. http://www.cdc.gov/cdctv/injuryviolenceandsafety/break-silence-stop-violence.html. This video shows how to recognize and stop dating violence.

"How Groups Help Chronic Illness and Pain." YouTube video, 5:53. Posted by "American Group Psychotherapy," April 10, 2013. https://www.youtube.com/watch?v=4mf0Igunm_M. Ann Steiner discusses how group therapy can work for people with chronic illness and pain.

"I Just Got on That Rail and Turned Around." *NPR StoryCorps*. Accessed May 27, 2015. http://storycorps.org/listen/kevin-briggs-and-kevin-berthia-150306. When Kevin Berthia climbed over the railing of the Golden Gate Bridge to jump to his death, California Highway Patrol officer Kevin Briggs talked him down. In this brief audio recording, they meet to talk about the event several years later.

"Layers of Identity in Mental Health—Crayons in the Hospital." YouTube video, 7:16. Posted by "Amanda Lipp," February 17, 2015. https://www.youtube.com/watch?v=pbdjnw_LFEg. During Amanda's stay in a psychiatric hospital after a suicide attempt, staff gave her crayons as a way to express her feelings. The medium became her voice—the bridge between her feelings and how she identified with them. Amanda is now a public speaker, advocating for mental health issues, as well as a filmmaker and artist.

A New State of Mind: Ending the Stigma of Mental Illness. 56:46. Televised on KVIE (CA) Public Television, May 30, 2013. http://vids.kvie.org/video/2365021031/. Narrated by actress Glenn Close, this documentary looks at the far-reaching effects of stigma associated with mental illness.

"Recommended Videos." American Association of Suicidology. Accessed [tk]. http://www.suicidology.org/resources/recommended-videos#NotRecommended. This site features a list of videos for teens related to suicide and mental health issues.

Veterans Health Administration. "Veterans Crisis Center—behind the Scenes." YouTube video, 8:29. Posted by "David Covington," January 26, 2012. https://www.youtube.com/watch?v=wH0gpp_WMkQ.
This film features a behind-the-scenes look at the VA call center in Canandaigua, New York. The film won the 2015 Oscar for best short documentary.

Websites

Alliance of Hope for Suicide Loss Survivors
http://www.allianceofhope.org
This nonprofit organization which assists people who have lost loved ones to suicide has been endorsed by leading suicide and mental health organizations. It has eight thousand members, 180,000 commentaries, a blog, a forum, memorials, and extensive resources for suicide survivors.

American Association of Suicidology
5221 Wisconsin Avenue NW
Washington, DC 20015
(202) 237-2280
http://www.suicidology.org
The mission of this organization is to understand and prevent suicide, promote research and training in suicidology, and to compile and disseminate information on suicide prevention to the public.

American Foundation for Suicide Prevention
120 Wall Street, 29th Floor
New York, NY 10005
(888) 333-2377
http://www.afsp.org
The organization's goal is to prevent suicide by funding research, advocating for public policy, creating educational programs for public about mood disorders and suicide, and supporting survivors.

National Action Alliance for Suicide Prevention
1025 Thomas Jefferson Street NW, Ste. 700
Washington, DC 20007
(202) 572-3784
http://actionallianceforsuicideprevention.org
This organization is a public-private partnership to advance suicide prevention by championing the US surgeon general's National Strategy for Suicide Prevention of 2012. The goal is to save twenty thousand lives in five years.

National Alliance on Mental Illness (NAMI)
3803 N. Fairfax Drive, Ste. 100
Arlington, VA 22203
(800) 950-6264 (helpline)
http://www.nami.org
NAMI is the nation's largest grassroots mental health organization dedicated to building better lives for the millions of Americans affected by mental illness. NAMI educates the public as well as mental health professionals and helps shape public policy for those with mental illness.

National Suicide Prevention Lifeline
(800) 273-8255 (routes call to nearest crisis center)
http://www.suicidepreventionlifeline.org
With a network of 163 crisis centers in forty-nine states, the National Suicide Prevention Lifeline provides contact with skilled, trained crisis workers twenty-four hours a day, seven days a week. The counselors want to help people find their reason to keep on living. The lifeline offers help to people with friends or loved ones threatening to harm themselves. The site also provides information specific to young people and veterans. Calls are confidential and free.

Pacer's National Bullying Prevention Center
8161 Normandale Blvd
Bloomington, MN 55437
(888) 248-0822
http://www.pacer.org/bullying
This organization promotes social change so that bullying is no longer considered an accepted activity. It provides resources for students, parents, and educators, and offers separate websites for teens and middle grade students about how to recognize and defuse bullying.

Stop Bullying.gov
200 Independence Avenue SW
Washington, DC 20201
http://www.stopbullying.gov
The US government's website on bullying offers extensive information about cyberbullying, recognizing it, and preventing and responding to it. It also provides videos about bullying, and a table called "Get Help Now" to help people understand what to do in specific circumstances.

Substance Abuse and Mental Health Services Administration (SAMHSA)
1 Choke Cherry Road
Rockville, MD 20857
(877) 726-4727
http://www.samhsa.gov/veterans-military-families
SAMHSA is the agency within the US Department of Health and Human Services that leads public health efforts to advance behavioral health of the nation. SAMHSA's mission is to reduce the impact of substance abuse and mental illness on America's communities. It has two dozen or more sections, including information about suicide prevention, resources for the military, bullying, and many other aspects of mental health and substance abuse.

US Department of Veterans Affairs
810 Vermont Avenue NW
Washington, DC 20420
(800) 273-8255 (Veterans Crisis Line)
http://www.mentalhealth.va.gov/suicide_prevention
On this site, the Veterans Affairs offers extensive resources to veterans, service members, and their families intended to prevent suicide by recognizing the warning signs and obtaining needed help. It provides specialized resources for mental health providers and discusses the use of the Veterans Crisis Line.

INDEX

PHOTO ACKNOWLEDGMENTS

The images in this book are used with the permission of: © iStockphoto.com/ Milanares, p. 1 (blue backgrounds); © iStockphoto.com/Fotana (ripped paper); © iStockphoto.com/Gordan1 (grunge frame); © iStockphoto.com/upheaval (border); © Diane Diederich/Vetta/Getty Images, p. 4; © Laura Westlund/ Independent Picture Service, pp. 7, 22, 25, 32, 48, 60; © Bill Cheyrou/Alamy, p. 13; Courtesy of Chris Crutcher, p. 14; © Tom Grill/Blend Images LLC/ Getty Images, p. 24; © iStockphoto.com/Linda Kloosterhof, p. 32; Don Feria/ AP Photo for Each Mind Matters, p. 43; Courtesy of e.E. Charlton-Trujillo , p. 50; Kevin Dietsch/UPI/Newscom, p. 54; © Win McNamee/Getty Images, p. 57; © iStockphoto.com/sturti, p. 63; U.S. Army Photo by Stephen Baker/U.S. Army Garrison Fort Lee, p. 65; © David Corby/Wikimedia Commons (CC BY-SA 3.0), p. 72; AP Photo/PRNewsFoto/Compassion & Choices, p. 76; © Tom Merton/ Caiaimage/Getty Images, p. 84; Courtesy of Amanda Lipp, p. 89; Richard B. Levine/Newscom, p. 93.

Front cover: © iStockphoto.com/Milanares (background); © Michal Szota/E+/Getty Images (bridge).

ABOUT THE AUTHOR

Connie Goldsmith has written numerous nonfiction books for middle school and upper-grade readers and has published more than two hundred magazine articles for adults and children. An active member of the Society of Children's Book Writers and Illustrators and of the Authors Guild, Goldsmith is also a registered nurse with a Bachelor of Science degree in nursing and a Master of Public Administration degree in health care. She writes a child health column for a regional parenting magazine in Sacramento, California, where she lives.